Supporting the Workplace Learning of Vocational and Further Education Teachers

Supporting the Workplace Learning of Vocational and Further Education Teachers is written to help people understand the arrangements in a workplace that enable and constrain teacher learning – and then to do something about it. It provides an accessible, research-based, and practical guide to making changes in the workplace to enable teacher learning.

The book illustrates approaches to supporting workplace learning through the extensive use of vignettes from real teachers and real teaching workplaces. With a focus on mentoring as an important component of teacher learning, it introduces the concept of a trellis of practices together with approaches for developing arrangements in the workplace that support teacher learning. It also examines the spaces between the personal and the professional and how these can become Communicative Learning Spaces where professional learning occurs.

The strategies and ideas provided in this book can be implemented at a whole-of-organisation, teaching department, small team, or individual level. An essential resource for Vocational Education and Training (VET) and Further Education (FE) teachers and managers, as well as others who support teacher learning in the workplace, this book is written to help make a difference.

Susanne Francisco is a researcher and teacher. Her background includes teaching in vocational education, supporting worker learning in large organisations, and working with teachers to support their ongoing learning. Susanne's research focus includes: workplace learning; the learning of teachers, academics and education leaders; professional learning; leading learning; and mentoring.

"If only this book had been around when I began my TAFE career, and especially when I was managing a team of both experienced and new teachers. Its theoretical underpinnings, supportive 'nuts and bolts' suggestions, and the vignettes telling stories from a wide range of practitioners and work sites, keep it very real. It also has one of the best concluding chapters I have read in a nonfiction book, in that it provides an overall moral and ethical framework that will inspire action."

Denise Newton, *former TAFE practitioner and leader*

"This book provides a solid foundation for those seeking to support teacher learning. I found it a delight to read: it flows well, is easy to understand, and provides a multi-faceted approach by addressing the ideas in a range of ways including through teacher stories, an overview of relevant research, and discussion of possible strategies. I particularly like the way the author 'speaks' to the reader. As I was reading, I found myself planning how to put the ideas and strategies in place in my own context."

Tracey Dodimead, *VET teacher, manager and leader of teacher learning*

Supporting the Workplace Learning of Vocational and Further Education Teachers

Mentoring and Beyond

Susanne Francisco

Routledge
Taylor & Francis Group
LONDON AND NEW YORK

Cover image: © Getty images

First published 2022
by Routledge
4 Park Square, Milton Park, Abingdon, Oxon OX14 4RN

and by Routledge
605 Third Avenue, New York, NY 10158

Routledge is an imprint of the Taylor & Francis Group, an informa business

© 2022 Susanne Francisco

The right of Susanne Francisco to be identified as author of this work has been asserted in accordance with sections 77 and 78 of the Copyright, Designs and Patents Act 1988.

All rights reserved. No part of this book may be reprinted or reproduced or utilised in any form or by any electronic, mechanical, or other means, now known or hereafter invented, including photocopying and recording, or in any information storage or retrieval system, without permission in writing from the publishers.

Trademark notice: Product or corporate names may be trademarks or registered trademarks, and are used only for identification and explanation without intent to infringe.

British Library Cataloguing-in-Publication Data
A catalogue record for this book is available from the British Library

Library of Congress Cataloging-in-Publication Data
Names: Francisco, Susanne, author.
Title: Supporting the workplace learning of vocational and further education teachers: mentoring and beyond / Susanne Francisco.
Description: Abingdon, Oxon ; New York, NY: Routledge, 2022. | Includes bibliographical references and index. |
Identifiers: LCCN 2021047984 (print) | LCCN 2021047985 (ebook) | ISBN 9780367632540 (hardback) | ISBN 9780367632564 (paperback) | ISBN 9781003112624 (ebook)
Subjects: LCSH: Vocational teachers–In-service training. | Adult education teachers–In-service training. | Mentoring in education.
Classification: LCC LB1736 .F72 2022 (print) | LCC LB1736 (ebook) | DDC 374/.013–dc23/eng/20211213
LC record available at https://lccn.loc.gov/2021047984
LC ebook record available at https://lccn.loc.gov/2021047985

ISBN: 978-0-367-63254-0 (hbk)
ISBN: 978-0-367-63256-4 (pbk)
ISBN: 978-1-003-11262-4 (ebk)

DOI: 10.4324/9781003112624

Typeset in Optima
by Newgen Publishing UK

This book is dedicated to the Vocational and Further Education teachers who have a passion for teaching. What you do makes a difference: for the students you work with, for your colleagues, for your communities, and beyond.

Contents

List of figures	xi
List of tables	xii
Acknowledgements	xiii

1	**Teacher learning in the workplace**	**1**
	Who is this book for and why is it needed?	3
	Learning in the workplace	4
	Learning how to go on	6
	The research underpinning the ideas in the book	7
	The theory of practice architectures	8
	Vocational and Further Education teachers as dual professionals	8
	Overview of the chapters	8
	How to read this book	10
	Questions to consider	11
	References	11
2	**Vocational and Further Education teacher vignettes**	**14**
	Introduction to the research	14
	Meeting the teachers – introductory vignettes	15
	Introducing the permanently employed teachers – from the research	16
	Introducing the casually employed teachers – from the research	23
	Concluding comments	29
	Questions to consider	29
	References	29

Contents

3	**Teachers learning how to go on**	**31**
	What novice teachers learn	32
	What experienced teachers learn	34
	Introduction to how teachers learn through undertaking their role as a teacher	37
	Introduction to a trellis of practices that support learning in the workplace	40
	Questions to consider	40
	References	40
4	**Workplace arrangements that enable and constrain teacher learning**	**43**
	Why is a theory relevant here?	43
	The theory of practice architectures	44
	Cultural-discursive arrangements	45
	Material-economic arrangements	47
	Social-political arrangements	51
	Practice architectures that enable and constrain teacher learning in the workplace	54
	Individual agency	68
	Concluding comments	70
	Questions to consider	70
	Further reading	72
	References	72
5	**A trellis of practices that support learning: more than mentoring**	**75**
	Practices that support learning (PSLs)	75
	A trellis of practices that support learning (PSLs)	76
	Concluding comments	87
	Questions to consider	88
	Further reading	88
	References	89
6	**Mentoring**	**90**
	Induction mentoring	91
	Developmental mentoring	95
	Developing the structures for successful mentoring	98
	Mentoring and adult learning principles	99

	Phases of a mentoring relationship	101
	Further considerations	104
	E-mentoring	104
	Mentors specialising in particular areas	106
	Peer group mentoring (PGM) – Finnish style	107
	Supervisors as mentors	107
	Developing the capability to mentor others	108
	Useful skills and characteristics for mentors	108
	Practice architectures that enable and constrain mentoring	111
	Concluding comments	111
	Questions to consider	112
	Further reading	112
	References	113
7	**Learning in in-between spaces: creating communicative learning spaces**	**115**
	In-between spaces	115
	Creating in-between spaces	123
	Increasing possibilities for in-between spaces to become communicative learning spaces	126
	The fragility of communicative learning spaces	131
	Conclusion and summary	135
	Questions to consider	136
	References	136
8	**Leading learning: building a trellis of practices to support professional learning**	**138**
	Leading learning	138
	Enabling teacher agency	140
	Trellis of practices that support learning (PSLs)	141
	Changing the practice architectures of a site	143
	Action research	144
	Leading the learning of casually employed teachers	147
	Leading the learning of experienced and accomplished teachers	153
	Reflective practice	158
	Survey of your local site	161
	Concluding comments	165
	Questions to consider	165

Contents

	Further reading	166
	References	166
9	**So what, now what: where to from here?**	**168**
	Key messages	168
	Developing praxis	173
	Now what? Where to from here?	175
	Concluding comments	179
	Questions to consider	180
	Further reading	180
	References	181
Index		182

# Figures

5.1	Sarah: limited inter-related PSLs	78
5.2	Sam: a trellis of PSLs in the Design Department	79
5.3	Tamsin: an online trellis of PSLs	83
5.4	Alice: a trellis of PSLs with two mentors	84
5.5	Ewan: a strong trellis of PSLs	86

Tables

5.1	Sam: examples where PSLs inter-relate	79
6.1	Mentor skills and characteristics	108
8.1	Deliberately supporting casual teacher learning	150
8.2	Deliberately supporting experienced teacher learning	155
8.3	Site survey questions	161

Acknowledgements

My first thanks need to go to the teachers who participated in the research projects that form the basis of this book. I am both grateful for, and inspired by, what you have shared with me.

My heartfelt thanks to two vocational education practitioners and leaders – and friends – who provided critical feedback on earlier drafts of this book: Denise Newton and Tracey Dodimead. Their constructive advice about the ideas in the book, and about how these ideas were framed, has been invaluable. I am very grateful for the time, energy, and ideas that they have contributed to the development of this book. Thanks also to Nina Storborg for suggestions related to the first chapter of the book, and for discussions about teacher learning and teacher support for the learning of others.

My thanks also to the Pedagogy Education and Praxis research groups for ongoing discussions about learning, teaching, praxis development, power, solidarity, and the theory of practice architectures. Special thanks to those who have collaborated on research and writing projects with me, including Stephen Kemmis, Kathleen Mahon, Christine Grice, Anette Forssten-Seiser, Lill Langelotz, Mervi Kaukko, Ela Sjølie, Oriana Price, Amanda Lizier, Gunilla Karlberg-Granlund, Rachel Jakhelln, Christine Edwards Groves, Ingrid Henning Loeb, Petri Salo, Michaela Pörn, Anette Olin and Jane Wilkinson. You are inspiring, collegial, fun to work with, and so much more: and you make such a difference.

One of the research projects that informs this book was undertaken as a PhD at the University of Technology Sydney (UTS). I am grateful that the university covered PhD tuition costs. My wholehearted thanks to my research supervisors David Boud and Gregory Martin for their wisdom, guidance, and support throughout the PhD journey and beyond.

Acknowledgements

Thanks also go to Mark Filmer for the careful and professional editing throughout the book. Mark has gone above and beyond to provide valuable and timely feedback, sometimes with tight turnaround times. He truly is a professional.

My deepest thanks go to Michael Fiveash who has lived the journey with me throughout the writing of the book and the related research that informs the book (and in life in general); who has graciously read every chapter many times, and made valuable suggestions along the way. I couldn't do this without you.

Teacher learning in the workplace

I love teaching in VET. I'm doing it because I do love it and I feel like I've found my place.

Maria, Business teacher

I want to give the students as much as I can so they can go out confidently and do a great job and be fulfilled and happy. And for the employer, so they can be absolutely confident that, if they employ that person, they know what they are doing. I would have been a teacher for all my life if I'd known how nice and intellectually stimulating it is.

Michael, Horticulture teacher

The biggest emotion I feel in my teaching is the pride that I feel for the students. You know, when they physically create something practical, or when I set them tasks to deliberately challenge them, and they meet the challenge. So, a lot of pride there. I really enjoy it; I'm really happy doing it.

Ewan, Air Conditioning and Refrigeration teacher

I'm passionate about teaching…I love working out how to engage disengaged students, and to make a difference to their lives.

Tamsin, Foundation Studies teacher

The Vocational Education and Training (VET) and Further Education (FE) teachers who I have interacted with as a colleague, teacher, and researcher usually have one key thing in common – they are passionate about their

DOI: 10.4324/9781003112624-1

work. Most have a passion for their teaching area, for teaching more broadly, and usually for both. A large majority are also eager to continue to learn and develop throughout their teaching career.

VET and FE teachers are a unique group of people. They are usually dual professionals who have already been successful in their first occupation – the one that they are teaching about. I have never met a VET or FE teacher, manager, or leader who didn't have an interesting background. This background is one of the things that they draw on as teachers, managers, mentors, and leaders. These experiences also form the stepping off point for ongoing learning and development.

The VET and FE sectors are large, rapidly changing, and complex. These complexities are impacted by many factors, including high employer, student, and community expectations; ongoing changes due to globalisation and internationalisation requiring increasingly sophisticated approaches; a competitive training 'market'; and ongoing changes to government policies that impact Vocational and Further Education both directly and indirectly.

VET and FE teachers face high expectations. They also work with a range of diverse student groups who have a broad range of abilities and needs. Students can range in age from 15 to more than 70. They can be full-time workers, casually employed workers, unemployed, or deliberately not engaging with paid employment. They can have a history of social and educational disadvantage or be from a privileged background. They can have a wide range of language, literacy, and numeracy skills, and they bring with them a range of learning skills and experiences. VET and FE teachers can be in sites (classrooms, worksites, workshops) where there is an overlap in these categories resulting in many diverse students in the same room (virtual and/or physical) at the same time. Sarah, a novice Business Administration teacher who participated in one of my research projects, characterised it as follows:

> *There is never one type of student, they are all individual. You can't put them all in the same bucket; you could have 14 students and 14 buckets, they're all unique. They all have their personalities, they all have their writing styles, they all have the way that they act or respond in class. There are the ones with the "Yes, I know" sort of responses. And the ones that won't say a word all semester and you try desperately to [engage with] them. All students are different.*

We expect much of VET and FE teachers, perhaps more than we expect of any other group of teachers. To be able to fulfil the many roles and expectations that we have for VET and FE teachers we need to support their learning. Undertaking formal education is one important way that teachers learn to develop their teaching, assessment, and student support practices. Learning in the teaching workplace is another. These are not either/or options; both are crucial. And both require deliberate attention to ensure teacher learning is well supported. As Kersh (2015) argues, "Making a workplace a learning space has been considered one of the challenges of contemporary workplace development" (p. 847). This book focusses on how to support teacher learning in the workplace.

Who is this book for and why is it needed?

This book has been written for VET and FE teachers,[1] for those who support the learning of VET and FE teachers, and for others who support adult learning.

Much of the learning that people who support adult learning do takes place in the teaching workplace (Francisco, 2020a). This doesn't deny the important learning that takes place through education courses. Instead, it acknowledges that:

- many teachers begin teaching without a teaching qualification
- learning as a result of undertaking a teacher education qualification is enhanced through applying the learning in the workplace
- there are some things that can only be learnt in the workplace, including what is expected, in this place, at this time.

In research that Billett et al. (2014) undertook across four different industries, the researchers found that "the manager's view of assistance for learning is largely comprising training programs" (p. 22). This single focus on attending training programs to support worker learning is despite decades of research that has highlighted the crucial value of learning in the workplace (see,

---

[1] Researchers in this area have found that the title used for people who teach VET and FE is an area of contention, with people often having a strong view about what these people should be called. Options include teacher, trainer, facilitator, lecturer, and practitioner. I have used the term 'teacher' throughout this book.

for instance, Billett, 2001; Fuller & Unwin, 2004; Lave & Wenger, 1991). It shows that Eraut's (2004) argument that there is a lack of understanding "about how much learning does (and how much more learning might) take place on the job" (p. 271) continues to hold. It is timely to have a book that focusses explicitly on supporting the workplace learning of teachers.

This book addresses questions such as:

- *What do VET and FE teachers learn in the workplace?*
- *What arrangements in the workplace support teacher learning?*
- *How can mentoring support teacher learning?*
- *How can you support your own workplace learning?*
- *How can you support the workplace learning of teachers?*

Learning in the workplace

People learn through formal education courses before entering an occupation or a profession, formal education courses while working in an occupation or profession, as well as other forms of continuing professional learning. Nonetheless, a large proportion of worker learning happens in the workplace (Billett, 2001; Eraut 2004, 2007; Francisco, 2020b).

The environment within a workplace has a profound effect on what happens there. What is done, what is said, and the relationships between people are significantly impacted by different aspects of the teaching workplaces in which VET/FE teachers operate. This includes the languages and specialist discourses that shape people's understanding and thinking, the material environment that shapes what they can do and what resources and facilities will be available to them, and the social environment that shapes the roles and relationships between people in the workplace.

For some time, the workplace has been identified as an important place for learning, and for most VET and FE teachers the workplace forms a crucial part of their learning about being a teacher. Much of what VET and FE teachers learn about their role as a teacher takes place after they begin in that role. For some, the workplace is the only place for learning about their teaching role. And, yet, the workplace is not always set up in such a way that it supports learning. Hobson et al. (2015) note:

> There is evidence that in some FE settings the workplace learning of teachers is limited due to the workplace culture, organisational

systems and processes and the allocation and structuring of work. In addition, some staff are isolated from support due to the location of their work, part-time working and/or being the only subject expert in their team.

(p. 23)

I found similar issues in my research (Francisco 2017, 2020b).

Simply being in the workplace and doing the job does not necessarily result in learning (Billett, 2001). Sometimes the workplace can even be set up in such a way that it constrains teacher learning. Drawing on studies by Lucas and Unwin (2009), Maxwell (2010, 2014), Orr (2012), and Orr and Simmons (2010), Hobson et al. (2015) argue "Reports and peer reviewed papers draw attention to the ways in which FE and Skills sector workplaces often impede the learning of both beginner and experienced teachers" (p. 10). With high expectations and high demands on VET/FE teachers, and decades of research showing the value of well-supported workplace learning, it is incumbent on organisations to create arrangements in the workplace that enable rather than constrain teacher learning.

Research (and if you have been working in VET or FE for a while, probably your own experience) reveals that the roles and practices that VET/FE teachers undertake vary considerably. Some of the variations are revealed in the vignettes developed throughout this book. Perhaps more than any other field of education, VET and FE are changing rapidly. This rapid change has been ongoing for some years, even decades, and even experienced teachers need to continually develop their practices.

Brennan Kemmis and Green (2013, p. 104) outline what they refer to as "a snapshot of the role" of a VET teacher:

- equip individuals with broad-based skills and knowledge;
- prepare diverse learners for the modern labour force, and to adopt new and valued approaches to skill development;
- demonstrate industry currency and develop close partnerships with industry, so education and training are closely linked to industry needs;
- more effectively link formal, non-formal, and informal learning;
- facilitate the movement of workers with low skill levels to higher skill levels;
- improve levels of participation of those with low skill levels;
- tailor provision to the distinctive needs of enterprises.

There are several such lists (and some are much longer); suffice it to say here that VET/FE teachers at a minimum need to learn to undertake at least the relevant teaching, assessment (and often pastoral care) practices that are appropriate in their local site. It is not surprising that being a teacher in VET and FE can be demanding and complex. It requires a high level of skill and ongoing development to be done well. As Wheelahan argues, "The contexts VET teachers work in, the students they teach, and the qualifications they deliver are more diverse than those in higher education or schools" (2010, p. 9). She goes on to argue further that "the demands on VET teachers are more complex than either schools or higher education" (p. 11). To be able to undertake these roles, Brennan Kemmis and Green (2013, p. 104) argue that:

> The VET professional will need more than ever to be autonomous, independent, critical, appreciative of the broader social and civic goals of education and training, and a VET professional who is intellectually gymnastic and able to cope in new and different arrangements and with new and different students.

The arrangements in the workplace that can support and maintain the development of such teachers are likely to vary from site to site.

In Australia (and other countries) there is a high level of teacher casualisation and short-term contracts. Well over a third of all Australian VET teachers are employed in this way (Knight et al., 2020). Other research shows that casually employed teachers have less access to professional development than permanently employed teachers (Guthrie, 2010). If casual teachers are to develop even adequate teaching skills, their learning needs to be clearly and deliberately supported. While focussing on the workplace learning of all teachers, this book also explicitly addresses approaches that support the learning of casually employed teachers.

Learning how to go on

The focus of this book is on teacher learning. But what do we mean by "learning"? Sometimes learning is understood to be confined to engaging in a formal education course. Learning does occur during formal education (if it didn't, we would all be out of a job). It also occurs in many other circumstances, including in the workplace.

Lave and Wenger's (1991) ground-breaking book *Situated Learning: Legitimate Peripheral Participation* led to a change in understanding of learning and how it happens. They provided examples from their research of learning taking place in workplaces and communities. A key contribution of their research was the development of an understanding that learning involves social interaction and engagement. Billet (2001) takes up this point, arguing that learning can be seen as "the product of participation in social practice through engagement in the activities and access to support and guidance" (p. 2).

One valuable way to consider learning is from the perspective of "learning how to go on" (Wittgenstein, 2009). That is, learning the practices that are most appropriate at this place and in this time, so that a teacher can be confident in saying, "Now I know how to go on" (p. 66). This "knowing how to go on" might be at a basic and practical level for novice teachers (now I know how to design an assessment task like the one that I was given as a model), and becomes more sophisticated and complex for accomplished teachers. As Dall'Alba (2009) argues:

> Learning to become a professional involves not only what we know and can do, but also who we are (becoming). It involves integration of knowing, acting and being in the form of professional ways of being that unfold over time.
>
> (p. 34)

Chapter 3 (Teachers learning how to go on) takes the ideas introduced in this section further.

The research underpinning the ideas in the book

The strategies and theories outlined in this book have been developed as a result of rigorous research. One of the research projects was a longitudinal study that involved nine teachers followed during their first two years of teaching. Another project involved experienced teachers working in a range of environments, including in small regional education organisations, large education organisations, and organisations where the main focus was not education, but the research participants had the role of supporting the learning of others in the organisation. These research projects are discussed in more detail in Chapter 2. You will see that other relevant research is also drawn on extensively throughout the book.

The theory of practice architectures

The research on which much of this book is based has been informed by the theory of practice architectures (Kemmis et al., 2014; Mahon et al., 2017). This theory foregrounds practices and the arrangements in each local site that enable and constrain particular practices. It provides a useful framework to consider approaches we can use to support teacher learning. The theory of practice architectures is outlined in Chapter 3 in more detail.

Vocational and Further Education teachers as dual professionals

VET and FE teachers are usually dual professionals. That is, they are teaching professionals, and they are professionals in the occupation or profession that they are teaching about (Orr, 2019). They must necessarily become skilled in both areas.

In Australia, most VET teachers begin their teaching role with training, experience, and expertise in their industry area. On starting as a teacher (and for the rest of their teaching career), they need to develop and continue to enhance their skills associated with their teaching role. They need to do this at the same time as they continue to maintain their currency and expertise in the industry that they are teaching about. In some other countries, the balance of expertise and experience when starting as a teacher is more tilted toward teaching skills, with less industry expertise. In both scenarios, ongoing teacher learning throughout their career is crucial to meet the high and ever-changing demands and skill needs of the VET sector.

Overview of the chapters

Chapter 2 introduces ten teachers whose stories are used throughout the book to illustrate key points. The quotes at the beginning of this chapter are from four of those teachers. The vignettes are drawn from research I have undertaken into the work-based learning of VET teachers. Each vignette introduces a particular teacher and the site in which they are working. Five vignettes feature teachers employed on a casual basis (that is, on a session-by-session basis – often referred to as 'sessional teachers'), and five feature teachers employed on a longer-term contract (at least 18 months) or permanently. The stories of these teachers are drawn on throughout the book in the form of brief vignettes to illustrate particular issues that teachers might encounter.

Chapter 3, called "Teachers learning how to go on", considers what it is that teachers do, what teachers learn, and how teachers learn through undertaking their work as teachers.

Chapter 4 identifies the key arrangements that impact teacher learning in the workplace. It does this by highlighting the broad range of site-based arrangements in the workplace, and by introducing the theory of practice architectures as a lens through which to better understand the site-based arrangements that enable and constrain teacher learning. These arrangements are illustrated by drawing on the vignettes.

Chapter 5 outlines the concept of *a trellis of practices that support learning* – that is, practices that inter-relate with each other, and, as a result of this inter-relatedness, provide greater support for teacher learning. Vignettes of specific sites that research participants were working in provide relevant examples to illustrate the concept.

Following on from Chapter 5, and the identification of the important part that mentoring can play in supporting teacher learning, Chapter 6 focusses on mentoring. The phases of a mentoring relationship are outlined, together with key actions for each phase. The chapter offers suggestions for developing mentoring capabilities for mentors, and for being a successful mentee. Finally, it outlines arrangements that can be put in place to support the mentoring of VET and FE teachers.

Chapter 7 introduces the concept of in-between spaces and outlines how learning can be supported in these spaces. In-between spaces are those spaces (physical and temporal) that are in-between the professional and personal, such as a timetabled shared morning tea, or colleagues sharing a car drive between campuses. The chapter provides an overview of learning in in-between spaces and uses the vignettes to illustrate learning in in-between spaces for VET teachers.

Chapter 8 focusses on leading learning in the teaching workplace. It begins by considering changed understandings of the concept of leading and what leading involves. Approaches you might use to evaluate the extent to which your existing worksite provides a *trellis of practices that support learning* are identified, and suggestions made for further development. This chapter also considers other issues relevant to leading teacher learning, including a section focussing on casual teachers, and another focussed on accomplished teachers. Reflective practice is also considered with suggestions for approaches that can be used to support reflective practice.

Chapter 9 concludes the book, making suggestions for where you might go from here in relation to supporting teacher learning (including your own) in your workplace. The chapter outlines possibilities for ways forward in establishing a trellis of practices that support learning in teaching workplaces in VET/FE at the levels of the whole organisation, a single teaching department, or with peers in a teaching team. The chapter also considers the concept of praxis and approaches that can be taken to support the development of praxis.

How to read this book

The short answer is – however you like. But a slightly longer answer might be of more use to you. We all have our preferred way to read a book. Some people want to have easy access to strategies and practical approaches. Some want to develop a strong understanding of the theory and research that underpins frameworks, strategies, and approaches. Others prefer a narrative where they can read a story that places the ideas and the strategies into a context. Some people want all of these. I have tried to provide all of these in this book. A strong use of sub-headings allows you to identify fairly quickly what each section addresses. The vignettes throughout the book tell the stories of real people who have experienced the things being discussed. If, when you start reading, you are not interested in being introduced to these teachers, you might choose to skip Chapter 2 initially, and perhaps come back to 'meet the teachers' later. If you are really interested in knowing more about mentoring, you might choose to start with Chapter 6. Similarly, if you are keen to know more about learning in in-between spaces, you could begin with Chapter 7. Many of the other chapters conclude with a "So what?" section, which teases out the purpose of the chapter and what you might do to make the most of what you have encountered in that chapter.

Questions to consider

At the end of each chapter, you will find some questions to consider in relation to the ideas in that chapter. The questions for this chapter are broad ones.

For the individual

- In what ways is your learning supported by the organisation that you are employed by?
- Consider your own workplace learning.
  - What has supported your learning in the workplace?
  - What has constrained your learning in the workplace?

For the organisation

- What existing arrangements support teacher learning in your organisation?
- Are there existing arrangements in some areas (or even across the entire organisation) that constrain teacher learning?

References

Billett, S. (2001). *Learning in the workplace: strategies for effective practice.* Crows Nest: Allen & Unwin.

Billett, S., Choy, S., Dymock, D., Smith, R., Kelly, A., Tyler, M., ... Beven, F. (2014). *Refining models and approaches in continuing education and training.* Adelaide: NCVER.

Brennan Kemmis, R. & Green, A. (2013). Vocational education and training teachers' conceptions of their pedagogy. *International Journal of Training Research, 11*(2), 101–121. doi: 10.5172/ijtr.2013.11.2.101

Dall'Alba. (2009). Learning professional ways of being: ambiguities of becoming. *Educational Philosophy and Theory, 41*(1), 34–45. doi: 10.1111/j.1469-5812.2008.00475.x

Eraut, M. (2007). Learning from other people in the workplace. Oxford Review of Education, *33*(4), 403–422.

Eraut, M. (2004). Informal learning in the workplace. *Studies in Continuing Education, 26*(2), 247–273. doi: http://dx.doi.org/10.1080/158037042000225245

Francisco, S. (2020a) What novice Vocational Education and Training teachers learn in the teaching workplace. *International Journal of Training Research.* Special

Issue: The site-based learning of VET teachers, *18*(1), 37–54. doi: 10.1080/14480220.2020.1747785

Francisco, S. (2020b). Developing a trellis of practices that support learning in the workplace. *Studies in Continuing Education, 42*(1), 102–117.

Francisco, S. (2017). Mentoring as part of a trellis of practices that support learning. In K. Mahon, S. Francisco, & S. Kemmis (Eds.), *Exploring education and professional practice – Through the lens of practice architectures*. Singapore: Springer.

Fuller, A. & Unwin, L. (2004). Expansive learning environments: Integrating organizational and personal development. In H. Rainbird, A. Fuller, & A. Munro (Eds.), *Workplace Learning in Context*. London: Routledge.

Guthrie, H. (2010). *Professional development in the vocational education and training workforce*. Adelaide: NCVER. Retrieved from www.ncver.edu.au/research-and-statistics/publications/all-publications/professional-development-in-the-vocational-education-and-training-workforce

Hobson, A. J., Maxwell, B., Stevens, A., Doyle, K., & Malderez, A. (2015). *Mentoring and coaching for teachers in the Further Education and Skills sector in England: full report*. London: Gatsby Charitable Foundation. www.gatsby.org.uk/uploads/education/reports/pdf/mentoring-full-report.pdf

Kemmis, S., Wilkinson, J., Edwards-Groves, C., Grootenboer, P., Hardy, I., & Bristol, L. (2014). *Changing practices, changing education*. Singapore: Springer.

Kersh, N. (2015). Rethinking the learning space at work and beyond: The achievement of agency across the boundaries of work-related spaces and environments. *International Review of Education, 61*, 835–851.

Knight, G., White, K., & Granfield, P. (2020). *Understanding the Australian Vocational Education and Training workforce*. Adelaide: NCVER. www.ncver.edu.au/research-and-statistics/publications/all-publications/understanding-the-australian-vocational-education-and-training-workforce

Lave, J. & Wenger, E. (1991). *Situated learning: legitimate peripheral participation*. Cambridge: Cambridge University Press.

Lucas, N. & Unwin, L. (2009). Developing teacher expertise at work: in-service trainee teachers in colleges of further education in England. *Journal of Further Education, 33*(4), 423–433.

Mahon, K., Kemmis, S., Francisco, S., & Lloyd, A. (2017). Introduction: practice theory and the theory of practice architectures. In K. Mahon, S. Francisco, & S. Kemmis (Eds.), *Exploring education and professional practice: through the lens of practice architectures*. Singapore: Springer.

Maxwell, B. (2014). Improving workplace learning of lifelong learning sector trainee teachers in the UK. *Journal of Further and Higher Education, 38*(3), 377–399.

Maxwell, B. (2010). Teacher knowledge and initial teacher education in the English learning and skills sector. *Teaching Education, 21*(4), 335–348.

Orr, K. (2019). VET teachers and trainers. In D. Guile & L. Unwin (Eds.), *The Wiley handbook of Vocational Education and Training*. Hoboken, NJ: Wiley.

Orr, K. (2012). Coping confidence and alienation: the early experience of trainee teachers in English further education. *Journal of Education for Teaching: International Research and Pedagogy, 38*(1), 51–65.

Orr, K. & Simmons, R. (2010). Dual identities: the in-service teacher trainee experience in the English further education sector. *Journal of Vocational Education and Training, 62*(1), 75–88.

Wheelahan, L. (2010). *Literature review: the quality of teaching in VET*. Melbourne: LH Martin Institute for Higher Education Leadership and Management, University of Melbourne. Retrieved from www.researchgate.net/profile/Leesa_Wheelahan2/publication/267716264_Literature_review_The_quality_of_teaching_in_VET/links/549ad02a0cf2b8037137133f.pdf

Wittgenstein, L. (2009). *Philosophical investigations* (P. M. S. Hacker & J. Schulte, Trans. 4th ed.). Oxford: Blackwell.

Vocational and Further Education teacher vignettes

It is in the doing, and in the practice, that much of what we learn makes sense. Throughout this book many of the ideas and strategies that are introduced are illustrated through the stories of teachers. These are stories about real people, in real workplaces. This chapter introduces you to these people and these workplaces. You are introduced to ten teachers (Vocational Education and Training [VET] teachers as well as Further Education [FE] teachers) who you will engage with throughout the book. As well as illustrating key points being made, or what ideas and strategies look like in practice, the vignettes also highlight the variety of teaching sites that VET and FE teachers might work in. You are also introduced to the research that these teachers took part in, and on which much of this book is based.

Introduction to the research

This book has been developed based on research evidence. This evidence comes from the relevant academic literature as well as drawing on several research projects that I have undertaken. In this next section, I briefly outline two main research projects on which the book is based. If you are not interested in the details of the research projects, you could skip straight to the section "Meeting the Teachers".

The two main research projects that inform this book were undertaken with VET teachers in Australia. One project focussed on novice VET teachers, and the other on experienced VET teachers and managers. Several smaller research projects that I have undertaken also inform the book. In addition, the book draws on relevant research projects undertaken by others in relation to FE practitioners in the UK as well as VET in Europe and

Scandinavia. More details about the two main projects informing the book are provided below.

How novice VET teachers learn to become teachers

The research project, *How Novice VET Teachers Learn to Become Teachers*, was a longitudinal, qualitative multi-case study project undertaken over the participants' first two years of teaching. The participants were nine novice VET teachers who had not had any previous experience as a teacher and had not undertaken any teaching qualifications before starting as a teacher. Data collection included interviews (which formed the primary data used), a field journal, responses to email questions, sketches made by participants, photos, and publicly available documentation (see for instance Francisco, 2017, 2020a, 2020b).

Leading Learning: Building a Trellis of Practices to Support Learning of VET Teachers

The research project, *Leading Learning: Building a Trellis of Practices to Support Learning of VET Teachers*, built on the earlier research and investigated approaches that VET practitioners and managers put in place to support teacher learning in the workplace. In this qualitative research project, VET practitioners and managers as well as FE teachers were invited to develop a trellis of practices that support learning (this concept is discussed in detail in Chapter 4). They outlined the arrangements in their workplace that already supported teacher learning, as well as any changes they had made or proposed to make. They were then interviewed 18 months to two years after they had provided this detailed outline to discuss what changes had occurred and how the workplace now supported teacher learning.

Meeting the teachers – introductory vignettes

Next is an introduction to the stories of the ten teachers that will be drawn on in a series of vignettes used throughout the book. The stories are divided into those teachers employed on a permanent or contract basis (with a contract for at least 18 months) and those employed on a sessional basis. The stories are divided this way as research (Francisco, 2020a) shows that, depending on the basis on which they are employed, teachers have different access to workplace arrangements that support their learning (discussed in more detail in Chapter 3).

The vignettes are based on teachers who were participants in my research, and the local sites where they were employed as teachers. The purpose of providing these vignettes is to illustrate the points being made in different sections of the book. It might be that you can see yourself, or teachers who you recognise, in some of the stories. It might be that your own story and the site where you work are quite different to the stories portrayed here. A key thing to take away is that VET teachers are varied and various, with different life stories, different work circumstances, and different enablers and constraints on their learning. Similarly, teaching departments are varied and various, with different histories and arrangements. By providing a range of teacher stories (including the sites where they work), I aim to show how the various issues discussed, and strategies identified, might, and have, played out in real life.

Here I introduce you to these teachers as though they are still working in the positions that they were in when they were involved in the research. Of course, many of these teachers are now doing quite different things, and the teaching departments continue to change and develop. In the following chapters, you will discover more about each of the teachers and the departments they teach in, as their experiences are shared to illustrate and explore something in the text. While the teachers and their colleagues who are mentioned are real people, some details have been changed, including all names, to ensure anonymity.

Introducing the permanently employed teachers – from the research

In this section, you will meet five VET teachers (participants in research projects that I undertook) who were employed in a permanent, or long-term contract, teaching position: Alice, Trevor, Ewan, Sam, and Simon. These teachers are from several different colleges with a range of campus and organisational arrangements.

Vignette 2.1 Introducing Alice and the Department of Community Services

The first thing you notice when you meet Alice is her big smile. Alice is employed by the Community Services school, which is within a faculty of health and wellbeing in a large VET college. She was initially employed on a short-term contract. Due to the illness of a long-term teacher, she was offered a 12-month contract, and then a short time after starting she gained a permanent position. Such a rapid move to permanent employment is unusual in Alice's faculty and was due to several factors including Alice's skills, knowledge, and willingness to learn, as well as her manager's desire to ensure a stable teaching team. There is a low level of casualisation in the Community Services teaching team, and low staff turnover.

Alice has a psychology degree. She had extensive and broad experience in community services before becoming a teacher. Spending any time in Alice's company makes you aware of her high level of empathy, her valuing of the community services industry, and especially her valuing of the people who work in this industry. She noted:

> I'm particularly passionate about helping people adjust to living and living well, and to me it's a way of honouring those people who choose to do that work.

She sees her students firstly as workers in the community services and community development industry and her goal is to support them in this work through teaching well and supporting their learning.

> I want to give them the strength that they need and the knowledge that they need, and I realise that they're also seeking something higher, from that experience of learning. So, they're seeking enthusiasm and joy and engagement, and the fact that you're in a classroom, they're seeking connection with likeminded people as well, so I want to facilitate that for them.

Vocational and FE teacher vignettes

The Community Services staffroom is made up of workstations (computers, desks, chairs) that are separated by grey partitions. The teachers are separated from each other because of these partitions, and you can only see each teacher if you are standing beside them in their workspace. In other staffrooms, this would be isolating and suggest a lack of collegiality. However, the staffroom avoids this because of the communal table (covered in a bright tablecloth), and beside a kitchen area, that is the focal point of the room. Teachers walk past the table when going to and from classes. There is always at least one person at the communal table, and usually several teachers are gathered at the table – drinking coffee, discussing work, having a chat, developing resources, creating assessment tasks, and so on. Talking (sometimes serious philosophical and meaning of life discussions, sometimes discussions about students and teaching, and sometimes personal discussions), and laughing are common sounds in this staffroom.

Vignette 2.2 Introducing Trevor and the Electronics Department

Trevor didn't plan to be a teacher. It was the job that was advertised when he was looking for work during a restructure at his previous place of employment. Trevor noted:

> I had family obligations, a mortgage etc., and they couldn't give me an answer, and I said, "Well…I need a steady job", so I … looked in the paper and this job was there, and I thought "I'll throw my hat in". I didn't plan to be a TAFE [Technical and Further Education] teacher.

After working in electronics for more than 30 years, Trevor was employed on a permanent basis directly from his role in industry. Trevor had an associate degree in electro-engineering, as well as a trade qualification. He had completed a Certificate IV in Training and

Assessment within the first year of teaching and had almost finished a Diploma in Training and Assessment by the end of his second year of teaching.

Trevor had no prior teaching experience or teaching qualifications, and he was also responsible for the administrative work associated with being the coordinator for a trade qualification. He credits his experience in the army as supporting him to have the resilience needed in his first two years in his role as a teacher and qualification coordinator. Because no-one had been undertaking the coordinator role for more than a year before Trevor's employment, there was a lot of work to do in this role. As a result, Trevor's focus for the first two years of employment was primarily on his coordination role (although on paper this made up less than half of his workload). He had to do this with no experience, very limited support, and no clear way to learn what was required. Some of the resources used in the department had been developed more than 30 years previously for quite different qualifications.

Trevor's department has a high staff turnover and a high level of casualisation. When Trevor was interviewed for his position as teacher and qualification coordinator, the teaching department included a Head of School, an administrative assistant, a technical officer, a storeman, several permanently employed experienced teachers, and several casually employed teachers. When he began his role less than two months later, there was no longer a Head of School, and most of the permanent teachers had resigned and not been replaced. Within six months of starting in the position, the administrative assistant and technical officer were also both no longer working there, and were not replaced, and the storeman was working part-time.

The Electronics Department has a large staffroom with many vacant desks. Most of the teachers are casually employed tradesmen (there are no women) who arrive in time for the class they are teaching and leave immediately afterwards. Before Trevor's arrival, the casual teachers did not have email or computer access and students had no way of contacting them except during class. As a result, Trevor had to field student queries for all the casual teachers as well as his already demanding roles. Getting computer and email access for the casual teachers was one of the things he organised in his first three months of being employed. In addition to the casual teachers, there are three permanently employed teachers in the department; however, they are focussed entirely on the higher-level qualifications that they were employed to teach. One of these teachers was employed at the same time as Trevor, one was employed the year before, and one was an experienced teacher and qualification coordinator. Although these teachers provide some camaraderie in the staffroom, in many ways Trevor is very isolated and has limited access to support his learning.

Vignette 2.3 Introducing Ewan and the Air Conditioning and Refrigeration Department

Ewan was a new father when I first met him, and I had seen the photo of his new baby within five minutes. His delight in fatherhood was tangible. Ewan is a trade teacher in air conditioning and refrigeration and began his teaching career with a two-year full-time contract. He joined a well-established teaching team with a history of limited staff turnover. Before becoming a teacher, Ewan had owned his own air conditioning and refrigeration business. He had a trade qualification and over the years had supported the learning of many apprentices in his business. Ewan's focus in his role as a teacher is to support students to become good tradespeople and good businesspeople. I have used the term 'people' but, in the two years of the research project, Ewan had no female students.

Most teachers in Ewan's team had completed a university-level teaching qualification, although this was no longer a requirement in the organisation in which they worked. Their learning from the teaching qualification had been further developed through experience and enhanced over time through daily discussions among the teachers about teaching and learning contextualised to the needs of their particular cohort of students. Ewan had completed a Certificate IV in Training and Assessment by the end of his first year of teaching.

The Air Conditioning and Refrigeration staffroom features an open-plan office with rooms available for meetings and collaborative work as needed (although a lot of the collaborative work seemed to also happen across the desks in the open-plan staffroom). Adjacent to the staffroom (which is shared with the Electrical teachers) is a large tearoom where all teachers meet each day from 10.00–10.30 for "smoko" (morning tea). Ewan's workplace was collegial and supportive.

Vignette 2.4 Introducing Sam and the Design Department

When Sam joined the Building Design teaching team on an 18-month contract, he and his family had recently moved to the city for his wife to undertake a new job. Sam had a private architecture business in their previous home city, and, when he first moved, he was still working on some of these projects. His focus in taking the teaching role was to be at home to pick up his children after school, to support his wife in her new position, and to continue with some architecture projects. Sam has architectural qualifications (bachelor's and master's degrees) and had completed the Certificate IV in Training and Assessment by the end of his first year of teaching.

The Building Design Department has a relatively low staff turnover and relatively low level of casualisation. There is an experienced Head of School and Head of Faculty who have been able to ensure good access to resources. The staffroom is set up so there is a series of individual workstations as well as three round tables of various sizes where groups of teachers often come together to work on collaborative projects. There is no shared tearoom, however, teachers wander over to the nearby coffee shop together for coffee each morning.

Sam's key focus in his teaching is to prepare Building Design students to be successful in their work. He believes that a key component of being a successful building designer is to be able to communicate well with all those on a building site, including builders, engineers, and architects.

Vignette 2.5 Introducing Simon and the Electronics Department

Simon is a passionate teacher who works hard to develop the best learning possibilities for students. He is a likeable person who highly values integrity and honesty. He deliberately chose to be a teacher (accepting a large salary reduction) to give back to his industry and to fulfil his Christian beliefs related to supporting others. Simon had worked in the electronics industry for 30 years before becoming a teacher. He had the equivalent of an Advanced Diploma in Electronics Communications, as well as several single university level subjects in mathematics and computing that he undertook to develop specific areas of knowledge relevant to his work. He also completed a Certificate IV in Training and Assessment within the first year of becoming a teacher. Simon is in the same Electronics Department as Trevor (Vignette 2.2), having joined shortly after Trevor. However, many of his experiences were quite different. He was employed to teach higher level qualifications and his student cohort and teaching approaches were quite different.

Like Trevor, Simon joined a different teaching department to the one that existed when he accepted the job. The department had recently lost quite a lot of staff, including the Head of School, had a high rate of casualisation, and was struggling for resources. Simon is working with an experienced coordinator as well as another permanently employed teacher. However, these people have a very heavy workload. Simon noted:

> There's almost no leadership at all now. Basically, the teachers are left to run the show as it is, and the coordinator has a lot of responsibility put on him. [He's] just so busy … just so snowed under. I just don't think that he's got much time to assist me.

When Simon was first employed, he became aware of important health and safety issues in the classrooms and with the equipment being used by students. He reported these issues (many relating to electricity and that he considered life threatening) but, when no action was taken, he spent many hours in his first months of employment working on the issues himself.

Introducing the casually employed teachers – from the research

In this section you will meet five VET teachers (participants in research projects that I undertook) who were employed casually on a sessional basis: Maria, Michael, Tabitha, Tamsin, and Sarah. These teachers were employed across a range of organisations with a variety of organisational arrangements.

Vignette 2.6 Introducing Maria and cross-campus teaching

Maria's enthusiasm for teaching and supporting others is apparent immediately. She is an experienced teacher who is employed on a casual basis and undertakes (at least) a full-time teaching load most semesters. She teaches across three campuses – A, B, and C. A and C campuses are about an hour's drive in opposite directions from campus B. Maria is not compensated for the time or cost of driving between the three campuses. Her teaching is primarily with adult Year 10, 11, and 12 students, and she also does some teaching in Business.

Maria is the only teacher in her specific teaching area on two of the campuses. On the third campus, her colleague is an experienced teacher who is reluctant to use technology (including email), is generally disgruntled, and is planning to retire "at any time". There are other teachers in the adult Year 10, 11, and 12 programmes on each of the campuses. All are employed on a casual basis and come and go for different classes, and there is little interaction between the teachers. Maria uses a hot desk on each campus and carries her resources with her from campus to campus.

Maria has completed a Bachelor of Adult and Vocational Education with a focus on language, literacy, and numeracy, and a Certificate IV in Training and Assessment. She has been advised that, in the TAFE [Technical and Further Education] organisation where she is employed, there is no possibility for teachers to be employed on a permanent basis (this is not the policy of the organisation more broadly,

Vocational and FE teacher vignettes

but it is how it works in the regional area where Maria is employed). Maria noted:

> My understanding is that there is no such thing as permanent employment for teachers through TAFE. We are all casual and that's it.

In the time between semesters when there is no teaching, Maria's supervisor arranges projects for her to undertake so that she continues to receive an income. Maria has a real dedication to teaching and supporting her students. Her desire to teach this group of students comes with a personal cost. She noted:

> My husband said to me numerous times, why didn't you just do secondary [i.e., train as a secondary school teacher]? You would have been better off. And he still says it to me today. Why didn't you just do secondary? You would have a better job and better employment prospects.

It becomes apparent when speaking with Maria that teaching adults is not just a job, it is a vocation. She is very aware of the poor work conditions and tenuous nature of her employment. Maria notes:

> There's always that thing that my job could be taken away tomorrow. It doesn't matter how well qualified I am, it doesn't matter that I'm building this reputation as a good practitioner, it can all be taken away tomorrow by a change in strategic direction, and – I hate the us and them attitude, but I really don't like the way that corporate [management] … their lack of consideration for the teachers is appalling and the way that we are employed I think is appalling.

Despite this, she goes on to say:

> But I love being there. As crappy as it is, I love being there.

In other writing I have referred to teachers such as Maria as "Favela Teachers" because of the poor conditions of their employment (see Francisco, 2020b).

Vignette 2.7 Introducing Michael and the Horticulture Department

Michael is a horticulturalist. This is his occupation and his life. He has completed a bachelor's degree in the field as well as a master's degree. Michael had also completed a Certificate IV in Training and Assessment by the end of his first semester of teaching. Michael's focus is to support students to become good horticulturalists, good employees, and good employers who are happy and fulfilled in their work. When I met him, he was writing a horticulture book. He had worked for more than two decades in the horticultural industry before becoming a teacher and he had supported the learning of many apprentices during that time.

The Horticulture Department has offices around the edges of a large room and a large communal table in the middle. The casual teachers' hot desks are also in this central area. Importantly, the Horticulture Department has a daily morning tea at 10.00 that all teachers attend. Michael highly values these morning teas. He notes:

> I make a big effort to be here for the morning tea break even if I'm not teaching at those times. Just to hear what they are doing. What's difficult for them. What they find nice. All their good and bad stories.

Michael is employed to teach for six hours a week – made up of three two-hour classes over three days a week. His goal is to be employed as a permanent teacher. The Horticulture Department has a strong permanent teaching staff as well as quite a large casually employed staff. Michael is aware that gaining permanency, or even a long-term contract, will be difficult. In the meantime, he is working several other casual jobs to enable him to also work as a teacher.

Vocational and FE teacher vignettes

Vignette 2.8 Introducing Tabitha and the Beauty Therapy Department

Tabitha's passion is make-up and supporting others to use it well. Every time I met Tabitha, she looked beautifully groomed, and much younger than her age. Tabitha is employed on a casual basis to teach make-up one night a week, but this is only a small part of her heavy load. She has three children, two of them teenagers, to whom she gives a lot of care and attention. She also has a full-time administrative job that she is not inspired by, and, importantly, she has a wedding make-up business that keeps her very busy most Saturday and Sunday mornings. The wedding make-up work is also her passion and joy.

Tabitha had successfully completed a Certificate IV in Training and Assessment by the end of her first year of teaching. However, as she noted, she did not retain a great deal from having undertaken the (compulsory) qualification. This was completely different to her learning during her Certificate IV in Make-up, which she describes with passion and excitement, and which was clearly a source of inspiration for her. Tabitha did her teaching at night and had very little interaction with other teachers.

The Beauty Therapy Department has a strong permanently employed teaching team as well as several casually employed teachers. The staffroom is made up of a series of partitions where the permanent teachers are in little boxes with an entry to each "box". The casual teachers have access to a hot desk workstation, which is at the other end of the staffroom and completely separated from the permanent teachers. The rate of turnover of casual teachers in this department is quite high.

In other writing I have referred to teachers such as Tabitha as "Fringe Teachers" because of their limited interaction with the VET college (see Francisco, 2020b).

Vignette 2.9 Introducing Tamsin and "Regional Campus"

Tamsin is an energetic, empathetic, committed, and experienced teacher. She has been employed to teach Foundation Studies four days a week at a regional campus. The campus is an hour's drive from where she lives. Tamsin is a problem solver who works tirelessly to overcome issues of isolation and limited resourcing at the campus where she works. Before undertaking this role, she had worked for some years on short- and long-term contracts in another teaching area at the campus in her hometown. Tamsin's role at "Regional Campus" is a trial to determine if an ongoing role is required and, if so, whether it is viable. She was initially employed on a six-month contract that was then extended to an 18-month contract. Tamsin is an experienced teacher, and she holds a Bachelor of Adult and Vocational Education with a specialisation in language, literacy, and numeracy.

Tamsin has a strong focus on helping her students develop skills and capacity to engage with the community and workforce. She is the only Foundation Studies teacher at Regional Campus. There are other teachers on this campus, but she has not been introduced to them, they are all in discipline-based staffrooms, and there are no opportunities to interact at places such as a coffee shop or canteen because these facilities are not available. Tamsin notes that for her:

> It's a bit of a little isolated bubble.

Tamsin has been placed in the middle of an open-plan administration office where there are no other teachers. She notes:

> I can tell you it's been a bit of a shock to the system because ... I've come from a [larger programme] with all the teachers in the one space and now I'm on my own and even my workspace – being in an open office but I sit amongst the administration staff because there wasn't anywhere to put me.

Vocational and FE teacher vignettes

While Tamsin has limited access to teachers at Regional Campus, she has found ways to manage her isolation. This includes an online network of Foundation Studies teachers that she meets with fortnightly. She also returns to the campus in her hometown and interacts with previous colleagues, even team teaching with one previous colleague from time to time.

Vignette 2.10 Introducing Sarah and the Business Administration Department

Sarah is employed on a casual basis to teach Business Administration in a Flexible Learning Centre. Her goal is to learn to be a good teacher. Having been a translator for her migrant parents since she was a very young child, Sarah's particular focus is to support migrant students, and she has strong skills in this area. She also has a goal of being valued for her work and achieving financial security. Sarah had had extensive experience in business administration some years previously. She left this work when she had her first child.

Sarah has completed a Certificate III in Business Administration and is studying for a Diploma at another campus of the same college. Her teaching load varies considerably from week to week with some weeks as low as six hours and others higher than a full-time load. However, her load is primarily about 9–14 hours of teaching a week. As a single parent of a young child, and with no other employment, this variable income presents some difficulties.

There is a relatively high level of casual employment in the Business Administration Department, together with a strong core of permanently employed teachers and those on short- and long-term contracts. The staffroom of the permanent teachers is in a separate building to the casually employed teachers, and Sarah's only contact with experienced teachers is with the person who team teaches with her, who is also her mentor. The casual teachers' staffroom is cramped and uninviting. It has two desks and several filing cabinets that contain outdated paper-based resources that no-one has got around to throwing away. Unsurprisingly, this staffroom is rarely used.

Concluding comments

These vignettes have provided a brief introduction to the teachers whose stories you will read about throughout the book. As is usually the case when you first come to meet someone, this is just a start to their stories. As you continue through the book, you will learn more about the teachers, their workplaces, and how their learning is enabled and constrained by certain arrangements in their workplaces. Because these stories are of real teachers working in real environments, there is a certain complexity and messiness about their experiences and the arrangements that they encounter. I have deliberately included this messiness to show what happens in real life rather than trying to provide a sanitised version of teachers' lives. If at any stage as you encounter these teachers throughout the book and have forgotten the context in which they are operating, you can return to these introductory vignettes as a reminder.

Questions to consider

For the individual

- Can you see yourself or your colleagues in any of the teachers you have been introduced to through the vignettes?
- In these vignettes, what arrangements can you see that support teacher learning?
- In these vignettes, what arrangements can you see that constrain teacher learning?

For the organisation

- Can you see aspects of your organisation in any of the vignettes?
- What arrangements can you see that support teacher learning?
- What arrangements can you see that might constrain teacher learning?

References

Francisco, S. (2020a). Work based learning through a trellis of practices that support learning. *Studies in Continuing Education*, 42(1), 102–117.

Francisco, S. (2020b). What novice Vocational Education and Training teachers learn in the teaching workplace. *International Journal of Training Research*. Special Issue: The site-based learning of VET teachers, *18*(1), 37–54. doi: 10.1080/14480220.2020.1747785

Francisco, S. (2017). Mentoring as part of a trellis of practices that support learning. In K. Mahon, S. Francisco, & S. Kemmis (Eds.), *Exploring education and professional practice – through the lens of practice architectures*. Singapore: Springer.

Teachers learning how to go on

One of the things that occurs when someone takes up a new role, or comes to a new workplace, is that they learn "how to go on" (Wittgenstein, 2009) in that role and workplace. This chapter provides an insight into how teachers learn "how to go on" in the teaching workplace. It begins with an overview of research into what teachers do. Next is a discussion of what novice teachers learn and then what experienced teachers learn. The chapter finishes with an introduction to the topic of how teachers learn in the workplace (a topic that is taken up in other areas throughout the book).

In the *How Novice VET Teachers Learn to Become Teachers* research project (outlined in Chapter 2), I looked closely at what each of the novice teachers participating in the study learnt to do in their first two years of employment as a teacher – and primarily they learnt to undertake the role of a teacher as it was understood in that place and at that time. Teachers usually begin by undertaking the following practices in their first six months of teaching: teaching (often with a separate focus on teaching theory in the classroom and 'practical' in the workshop), lesson preparation, the development of assessment tasks, and assessing student learning (Francisco, 2020a). However, this is not universal. For instance, one of my participants did no teaching at all for the first six months he was employed and instead focussed on assessment; other participants were undertaking roles within six months (Trevor and Alice for instance) that others did not even consider until the end of their second year (Francisco, 2020b).

Usually the things that teachers do (the practices that they engage with) become more extensive the longer they are employed as teachers (Francisco, 2020a). This extension of work roles is consistent with what researchers have found for other industries (see for instance, Eraut, 2011; Lave &

DOI: 10.4324/9781003112624-3

Wenger, 1991). After the first year of being employed as a teacher, teachers taking part in my research were also involved in several other teaching-related practices – primarily resource development, subject guide development, and using online learning platforms. By the end of the second year, some of the teachers were also undertaking coordination roles for entire qualifications, liaising with employers, teaching in the workplace (where an organisation contracts the college to tailor a qualification specifically for that organisation and to deliver it at the workplace), curriculum development, leading resource development, and mentoring novice teachers.

What novice teachers learn

At a broad level, novice teachers learn to become teachers mostly through learning to do the practices outlined in the paragraphs above. And they learn to do these things in the way the other teachers in their teaching department do them. Sometimes when someone says they are teaching, the stereotype is that they are standing in front of a classroom of students and telling them something, and sometimes new teachers think that this is what they are employed to do. For some teachers this is further informed by their experiences of being a student decades ago, where they might have experienced a similarly transmissive approach. It sometimes comes as a surprise to new teachers that teaching involves different practices in different sites and usually a range of practices in each site.

The people you were introduced to in Chapter 2 undertook a range of different practices when they were teaching. For many of them, this involved a focus on one particular approach, especially when they first began teaching. For Trevor, a large part of what he did when he was teaching involved writing notes on a whiteboard with students copying the notes into their workbooks. For Sarah, it meant moving from one student to another in a flexible learning classroom where students would take a number and wait until the teacher was available to provide individual support. Ewan's teaching involved several approaches including supporting students individually or in pairs in a classroom designed as a trade workshop. For another teacher in sport and fitness, one of the approaches he needed to learn involved running an aerobics session that had both students and clients, where the students were both doing the aerobics session and learning how to safely run an aerobics session. Tabitha mostly focussed on arranging for students to learn how to do make-up by putting make-up on the face of another student with the teacher moving from student to student to provide advice and encouragement. Michael used many approaches from the beginning, including walking through glasshouses with a group of 15 students to support them to determine the needs of the different plants they were passing (for instance water, soil, and fertiliser needs). With Alice, one often-used approach involved setting up a case study and then moving students into groups of three to consider some of the implications of the case study. Of course, this is just a small sample of the many things that teachers do when they are teaching, and most of the teachers mentioned above also did more than the practices outlined, even in the first few weeks of teaching. The notable point is that what each of the teachers did, at least initially, was heavily influenced by what others in their teaching team did.

In my research with novice teachers, many have told me (without being asked) how surprised they were by the amount of work that is involved in being a teacher – work that is additional to being in a classroom or workshop with students. This 'additional work' usually involved class preparation, resource development, administration related to enrolments and the recording of student achievement, and the development of documents that provide an overview of the course and assessment requirements (often referred to as subject guides or subject outlines). In a longitudinal study of English Further Education (FE) teachers, Bathmaker and Avis (2013) also found evidence of this surprise. One of their participants noted that, "the amount of preparation and paperwork came as a shock" (p. 740). I have included this information here to highlight that those new to teaching would benefit from early and explicit information about what is involved to support them in managing their workload. While casually employed teachers with commitments elsewhere can particularly benefit from this, it is valuable for all new teachers.

Interestingly, although all participants in my study had been employed to teach in an area where they had extensive experience, one of the first things they had to learn was the content that they were teaching. Before starting as a teacher, their industry understanding and knowledge were primarily related to what they needed to know to do their job. In the teaching role, the content they were teaching was always broader than this (and often had changed from when they were a student or they had forgotten some of what they were not regularly using), and so they needed to learn this broader content. Teachers often refer to this content as "theory" to distinguish it from "prac" – the more hands-on learning that students do. For instance, Simon noted after he had been teaching for about six months:

> I'm relearning a lot of the material myself. Because a lot of it is theory that you don't use, that I haven't used in my normal job, so I'm having to revisit theory that I haven't done for a long time.

In summary, novice Vocational Education and Training (VET) teachers learn much in the first two years of being a teacher. What they learn is influenced by the traditions of the teaching department and the site where they are teaching. It is also influenced by the traditions of the industry that they are teaching about, by their experiences, and by the expectations of the manager and colleagues in their teaching department. Chapter 4 discusses these influences and how they enable and constrain teacher learning. It is important to note here that casually employed teachers, who usually spend less time in the teaching workplace, have less access to support from colleagues, and usually have less access to professional development (Guthrie, 2010), tend to rely more on their own learning experiences to inform their teaching. This has implications for the use of current teaching approaches. Novice and casually employed teachers often benefit from focussed and deliberate interventions to support their learning to be a teacher. This is discussed in more detail in Chapter 8.

What experienced teachers learn

The previous section focussed on the learning of teachers in the first two years of being a teacher. In this section, the focus is on the learning of more experienced teachers, particularly those teachers who could also be considered to be "accomplished" (Shulman, 1987), noting that years of experience does not always result in increased capability, although it often does. For many accomplished teachers, learning in relation to the practices noted in the section above continues throughout their teaching career. For these teachers, the focus for learning is often related to fine-tuning areas of expertise or expanding capabilities. A relevant example that many teachers – both novice and experienced – were recently pushed into because of the COVID pandemic, was teaching online.

In the previous section, I noted that novice teachers usually learn to do what the other teachers in their department do. Accomplished teachers often go beyond what others in their department do, and often they must go outside their department to seek input into their ongoing learning. This doesn't suggest that all (or even most) learning takes place outside their workplace, just that external input is often involved. This might include a mentor, undertaking a relevant qualification, a guided research project (an action research project is a good example of this), a network that meets regularly with a specific focus, even a book that is designed to support teacher learning. To best support teacher learning, all of these "external inputs" will need to be developed and trialled in the context in which the teacher operates and usually adapted over time to be of most use in that context.

Accomplished teachers are often focussed on being a "good" teacher and developing their skills and approaches to better meet student needs. It is worth considering what being an accomplished teacher might involve. Smith and Yasukawa (2017) undertook research to determine what Australian VET teachers and students considered to be the skills and actions of a good teacher. Students valued teacher professionalism, including things such as being organised, prepared for classes, and providing good feedback. Pedagogical skills, identified as including things such as being able to support student motivation, providing clear explanations, using adult learning approaches, and providing differentiated learning, were also valued. Other important skills and attributes included strong subject knowledge, industry relevant experience, the ability to manage the poor behaviour of students, fairness, and the ability to manage a diverse classroom.

In Smith and Yasukawa's (2017) study, VET teachers highlighted the importance of differentiated learning to meet the needs of a diverse range of students, to "be prepared to adapt one's teaching approaches for each group of learners and each learner within a group in response to the range of cultural, linguistic, social and educational factors influencing each learner's engagement, motivation and successes in learning" (p. 33). A strong foundation in the industry they teach about was also seen as crucial, as was knowledge of, and capability with, a range of teaching approaches. These were both seen as important components of being able to be flexible and adapt to learner needs. Having a passion for teaching, for supporting student learning, and for the industry they are teaching about, was also highlighted.

Like the students, teachers saw being organised and prepared for classes to be important. Finally, an engagement in ongoing learning and development in both their teaching and industry area was considered a key part of a "good" teacher's professionalism.

There are also several capability frameworks that identify expectations of teachers. In relation to such approaches to understanding what makes good VET teaching, Schmidt (2021) argues:

> The sector's understanding of VET teaching, and in particular, VET managers' understanding, is predominately reductionist in its approach, characterised by a preoccupation with distilling the VET teachers' work into atomised lists of requisite, reproducible skills, knowledge and behaviours. This has led to the development of ever-more teaching capability frameworks, models and standards, in the pursuit of the most comprehensive or complete representation of the attributes required of the VET teacher.
>
> (p. 149)

Schmidt argues that while capability frameworks might be valued by some for evaluative purposes, there is a danger that they can result in an atomised approach to teacher professional learning with a narrowing of teacher skills and knowledge focussed just on regulatory requirements. Instead, Schmidt argues, that for the professional development of teachers a more holistic focus is valuable, with a concentration on "the importance of the individual teacher's characteristics and qualities and the impact that vocational education and their teaching activities had on the lives of students" (p. 160).

In the previous paragraph, and in other literature, the focus is often on the "good teacher". This implies that, if the teaching is not good, then it is the fault of the teacher. Chapter 4 makes a different argument, showing that the arrangements in each local site that enable and constrain teacher learning, as well as what they do and how they do it, can have a powerful impact on whether the teaching is good or not. So, while this section has highlighted some things that teachers and students have identified as being of value, it is useful to step back and consider not the individual teacher and their ability to do these things, but how the arrangements in each local teaching department support these practices.

Teachers learning how to go on

Introduction to how teachers learn through undertaking their role as a teacher

Much of this book addresses the question of how teachers learn through undertaking their role as a teacher, so this section is introductory. I want to be clear that I do not argue that learning in the workplace should replace more formal education programmes for teachers. Instead, I argue that much learning (for all workers, including teachers) does take place in the workplace and it is important to consider how this happens and how to better support such learning. Broader research into learning in the workplace is also relevant in relation to the learning of teachers. Billett and Smith (2014) note that workers learn through "(i) engagement in work activities, (ii) observing and listening, and (iii) 'just being in the workplace'" (p. 890). Similarly, Billett and Choy (2013) argue that learning in the workplace occurs primarily through "observation, mimesis (i.e., imitation) and practice" (p. 267). Further, Eraut (2011) found that workers learn "from the challenge of work itself" and "consultation within the working group" (p. 8). My research with teachers found similar influences on teacher learning in the workplace. The key things that teachers identified as supporting their learning were the support of colleagues and supervisors, existing resources as models (especially in the first year or so of being a teacher), student feedback, trial and error, team teaching, co-teaching (where two teachers teach the same curriculum in the same teaching semester but to different cohorts of students), reflection and reading (Francisco, 2017).

The support of colleagues has been known to be an important component of workplace learning for some time (see for instance, Billett, 2001; Eraut, 2011; Robson, 2006). The support of colleagues for VET and FE teachers can vary from basic ad hoc advice and responses to questions, to extensive mentoring. The availability of this support varies from site to site. Orr and Simmons (2011) found limited support from colleagues for the learning of trainee FE teachers in England. Several factors impact on the availability of such support, including the workload of experienced teachers, the level of casualisation, teacher turnover, and other factors such as staffroom layout and whether the teachers are teaching during the day or evening. This is discussed further in Chapter 4.

Teachers often identify "trial and error" as a key approach to support their learning. One of the teachers participating in my research (Simon)

37

referred to his early learning as being largely through trial and terror. Student feedback is important for teachers to determine whether what they are doing is working. Another teacher, Michael, identified what he refers to as "active" and "passive" feedback. He sees active feedback as including direct comments such as "good class", explicit comments about what is occurring in the classroom or students' own learning and related requests for assistance. He sees passive feedback in body language, levels of engagement, performance levels on tests and other activities, and comments or questions that reveal student understanding (or lack thereof).

Having access to well-designed, quality resources such as lesson plans, assessment tasks, and class resources is valuable for a couple of reasons. Well-designed resources usually provide a good framework for teaching. Importantly, they also provide a model for any new resources that teachers develop.

Team teaching can be singled out as a highly valuable approach that supports teacher learning. It enables the three key things that Billett and Choy (2013) highlight as being valuable for worker learning: observation, imitation, and practice. Robson (2006) also identified learning through observing others as being valuable in supporting the learning of FE teachers in Britain. Team teaching allows for the combination of observing another teacher teaching as well as "just doing it" themselves and listening to feedback from their team-teaching colleague. It is also usually (always for the teachers in my studies) accompanied by working together with another teacher to prepare lessons as well as debriefing and reflecting together after classes.

Because VET teachers are dual professionals (Orr, 2019), with a focus on being a teacher as well as remaining current in the industry they are teaching about, their ongoing learning is necessarily across these two broad areas. In research with Swedish Floristry and Hairdressing teachers, Gåfvels (2020) found that experienced teachers used a range of approaches to support their ongoing learning. In relation to ongoing learning in the industry they teach about, this included inviting industry representatives and inspiring guests to speak with them (and their students), as well as viewing relevant YouTube videos. Some teachers found their regular visits to the workplaces of students continued to support their learning in their vocational field. One interesting approach that some Floristry teachers engaged with involved undertaking training in another craft area (such as pottery) to support the ongoing development of their creativity. For development as a teacher, ongoing discussions and reflections with their colleagues were valuable. The Hairdressing teachers invited other teachers into their classes and took part in the classes of others when invited.

In other research with experienced Swedish teachers, Henning Loeb (2020) found that the teachers also used a range of approaches to support their ongoing learning. The participants in her research were highly accomplished teachers who had a deep knowledge and understanding of their teaching area, a university level VET teacher qualification, and had been working as a VET teacher for many years. Each participant continued to develop and transform their teaching approaches, trying new strategies to address the issues that they encountered. Henning Loeb notes that experienced teachers continue to face new challenges and ongoing changes in site-based conditions:

> Accomplished VET teachers continuously are involved in developing their teaching practice as praxis, in the sense that they act in the knowledge that 'their actions will have good and ill consequences for which they have sole or shared responsibility, and who, in that knowledge, want to act for the good' (Kemmis & Smith, 2008, p. 8). In different ways and in different circumstances, they are involved in creating conditions of possibility for learning, including their own learning despite challenging circumstances.
>
> (p. 80)

Each of the teachers in the Henning Loeb study could access support for their learning in different ways, with some able to work closely and collaboratively with other teachers to develop their own learning as well as the learning of their students. Some teachers were more isolated and found alternative approaches to their ongoing learning including attending university courses and research-based professional learning programmes.

In my research with experienced VET teachers, I found that the teachers used a range of approaches to support their ongoing learning. This included undertaking university-level qualifications, seeking new projects, reflecting with colleagues, observing other teachers, and working together with a group of colleagues to address an identified problem.

How teachers learn through undertaking the role of a teacher, and how this learning can be supported in the workplace, is addressed in various ways throughout this book, and especially in Chapters 4, 5, and 8.

Introduction to a trellis of practices that support learning in the workplace

Different arrangements in each site will affect what teachers learn and how they learn it. As a result, teachers learn different things in each site, and their learning is supported in different ways. The site-based arrangements that enable and constrain teacher learning are the subject of Chapter 4. These different arrangements often interact with each other, and in some sites these interactions can provide a strong trellis of practices that support teacher learning, which is a way of describing the inter-relationships between different learning practices. A strong set of inter-related learning practices can be a powerful support to teacher learning. This is the focus of Chapter 5.

Questions to consider

For the individual

- What practices do novice teachers in your workplace need to learn in their first year of teaching?
- What are some of the practices that accomplished teachers learn in your workplace?

For the organisation

- What practices do novice teachers in your organisation need to learn in their first year as a teacher?
    - How are they supported to do this?
- What are some of the practices that accomplished teachers in your organisation learn?
    - How are they supported to do this?

References

Bathmaker, A. M. & Avis, J. (2013). Inbound, outbound or peripheral: The impact of discourses of organisational professionalism on becoming a teacher in English further education. *Discourse: Studies in the Cultural Politics of Education, 34*(5), 731–748. doi: 10.1080/01596306.2013.728367

Billett, S. (2001). Learning in the workplace: strategies for effective practice. Crows Nest: Allen & Unwin.

Billett, S. & Choy, S. (2013). Learning through work: emerging perspectives and new challenges. *Journal of Workplace Learning, 25*(4), 264–276. doi: http://dx.doi.org.ezproxy.csu.edu.au/10.1108/13665621311316447

Billett, S. & Smith, R. (2014). Learning in the circumstances of professional practice. In S. Billett, C. Harteis, & H. Gruber (Eds.), *International handbook of research in professional and practice-based learning.* Dordrecht: Springer. Retrieved from http://site.ebrary.com/lib/csuau/docDetail.action?docID=10896874

Eraut, M. (2011). Informal learning in the workplace: evidence on the real value of work-based learning (WBL). *Development and Learning in Organizations: An International Journal, 25*(5), 8–12. doi: 10.1108/14777281111159375

Francisco, S. (2020a). What novice Vocational Education and Training teachers learn in the teaching workplace. *International Journal of Training Research*. Special Issue: The site-based learning of VET teachers, *18*(1), 37–54. doi: 10.1080/14480220.2020.1747785

Francisco, S. (2020b). Work based learning through a trellis of practices that support learning. *Studies in Continuing Education, 42*(1), 102–117.

Francisco, S. (2017). Mentoring as part of a trellis of practices that support learning. In K. Mahon, S. Francisco, & S. Kemmis (Eds.), *Exploring education and professional practice – through the lens of practice architectures.* Singapore: Springer.

Gåfvels, C. (2020). VET teachers' learning in feminised vocations – a comparative study of Swedish floristry and hairdressing teachers. *International Journal of Training Research, 18*(1), 55–67. doi:10.1080/14480220.2020.1747789

Guthrie, H. (2010). Professional development in the vocational education and training workforce. Adelaide: NCVER. Retrieved from www.ncver.edu.au/research-and-statistics/publications/all-publications/professional-development-in-the-vocational-education-and-training-workforce.

Henning Loeb, I. (2020). Continuously developing and learning while teaching second language students. Four storied narratives of accomplished VET teachers. *International Journal of Training Research, 18*(1), 68–83. doi:10.1080/14480220.2020.1747786

Lave, J. & Wenger, E. (1991). *Situated learning: legitimate peripheral participation.* Cambridge: Cambridge University Press.

Orr, K. (2019). VET teachers and trainers. In D. Guile & L. Unwin (Eds.), *The Wiley handbook of Vocational Education and Training.* Wiley: New Jersey.

Orr, K. & Simmons, R. (2011). Restrictive practice: the work-based learning experience of trainee teachers in English further education colleges. *Journal of Workplace Learning, 23*(4), 243–257. doi:10.1108/13665621111128664

Robson, J. (2006). *Teacher professionalism in further and higher education: challenges to culture and practice.* London: Routledge.

Schmidt, T. (2021). Teacher as person: the need for an alternative conceptualisation of the 'good' teacher in Australia's Vocational Education and Training sector. *Journal of Vocational Education & Training, 73*(1), 148–165. doi:10.1080/13636820.2019.1698646

Shulman, L. (1987). Knowledge and teaching: foundations of the new reform. *Harvard Educational Review, 57*(1), 1–23. doi:10.17763/haer.57.1.j463w79r56455411

Smith, E. & Yasukawa, K. (2017). What makes a good VET teacher? Views of Australian VET teachers and students. *International Journal of Training Research, 15*(1), 23–40. doi:10.1080/14480220.2017.1355301

Wittgenstein, L. (2009). *Philosophical investigations* (P. M. S. Hacker & J. Schulte, Trans. 4th ed.). Oxford: Blackwell.

Workplace arrangements that enable and constrain teacher learning

This chapter identifies the key arrangements that affect teacher learning in the workplace. It does this by highlighting the broad range of site-based arrangements in the workplace, and by introducing the theory of practice architectures as a lens through which to better understand the site-based arrangements that enable and constrain teacher learning.

A large proportion of learning to be a teacher happens in the teaching workplace (Francisco, 2020b). This is the case with many (probably all) occupations and professions (Eraut, 2004). As discussed in previous chapters, the arrangements that are present, or brought into the workplace (which can include a virtual workplace), affect worker learning (Lucas & Unwin, 2009). As Orr (2019) notes about research he undertook into the learning of new FE teachers in the UK, "much of the new teachers' opportunity to develop depended on the specific circumstances of their department or who their manager was" (p. 341). In research that I have undertaken in VET organisations, there were different arrangements that influenced teacher learning in every site. It is valuable to examine these arrangements and identify how they enable and constrain teacher learning. We use the theory of practice architectures to do this.

Why is a theory relevant here?

The perspective that we take about what is done and how it is done can open new ways of understanding – even when looking at the same things. There are a number of theoretical frames through which learning has been explored, and with many of these the focus has been on the individual and how well they learn (or not). Practice theories enable a focus on practice;

DOI: 10.4324/9781003112624-4

on what really happens and what it is that affects what happens (Nicolini, 2012). This chapter provides a more detailed discussion of the theory of practice architectures (introduced briefly in Chapter 1), and then uses the theory to identify the site-based arrangements that enable and constrain teacher learning in the teaching workplace. In this book, the environment in which learning is undertaken, and how well that environment enables or constrains teacher learning, is foregrounded. That doesn't mean that we ignore individual dispositions and capabilities. Individual agency is discussed toward the end of this chapter. It is also explored throughout the book and identified as an important component of teacher learning.

The theory of practice architectures

The theory of practice architectures is a site-based practice theory. It provides a framework for investigating how different arrangements that are present at, or brought into, a site enable and constrain the practices in that site. That is, it supports the exploration and analysis of what actually happens in a site. These arrangements are present in three dimensions: the cultural-discursive, the material-economic, and the social-political (Kemmis et al., 2014; Mahon et al., 2017). Each of these is briefly outlined below, developed further in the following pages, and then illustrated in the vignettes of VET teachers throughout the chapter.

The *cultural-discursive* arrangements prefigure,[1] but do not predetermine, the *sayings* in a site. That is, what is said (and thought about) in the site and the practices that are present in the site. This includes the type of language used (such as formal or informal), the topics of conversation, and the things that are said (Kemmis et al., 2014). For instance, in a site where Business Administration is being taught in a traditional classroom, the sayings will be different to those that might be present in a site where a Horticulture teacher might be supporting the learning of students in a public park. The language used, the topics of conversation, and what is said are all likely to be different.

---

1 For a visual image of something that is prefigured, imagine a meandering dirt path through a forest. The way that you would walk through the forest is prefigured by that path and you are most likely to follow it. But you could also walk into the forest away from the path; it might be more difficult to do so, but still possible.

The *material-economic* arrangements prefigure, but do not predetermine, the *doings* in a site. That is, what is done in the site. The material-economic arrangements include the physical arrangements in the site, the resources available, timetabling, and the employment arrangements for workers in the site (Kemmis et al., 2014). For instance, a Business Administration lesson being undertaken in a classroom is likely to have different physical arrangements – such as desks, chairs, an electronic whiteboard – to a Horticulture lesson being undertaken in a public park – such as the park, trees, shrubs, perhaps permission was required to take the class to the park.

The *social-political* arrangements prefigure, but do not predetermine, the *relatings* in a site. That is, how people relate with each other in the site. Social-political arrangements of power and solidarity affect relationships within the site (Kemmis et al., 2014). For instance, how the Horticulture students interact with the teacher and each other in the park might be different to how the Business Administration students interact with their teacher and each other in the classroom.

In the rest of this chapter, we use the theory of practice architectures to explore the workplace arrangements that enable and constrain teacher learning. The next sections discuss the cultural-discursive, material-economic, and social-political arrangements in more detail, and this is followed by vignettes that illustrate practice architectures in particular sites. As noted previously, the examples outlined here are of real sites, and real teachers (names are changed) in real situations.

It is important to note that while the chapter in many instances separately addresses the cultural-discursive, material-economic, and social-political arrangements, in reality they are inter-related. This separation is an analytical tool only to help us give greater consideration to, and gain a greater insight into, the different arrangements at the workplace and the impact these can have on teacher learning.

Cultural-discursive arrangements

The cultural-discursive arrangements influence the "sayings" in a site. Cultural-discursive arrangements that have the potential to affect teacher learning include the valuing of vocational education by employers, students, governments, and the community. The related discourse around the quality of Vocational Education, and the associated language used to refer to

Vocational Education teachers and students creates practice architectures that enable and constrain particular practices.

In a Vocational and FE site, the cultural-discursive arrangements usually include at least two different types of language: industry/occupation/profession-related language (hereafter referred to as industry language) and training-and-education-related language.

Industry language

Most vocational teachers are employed because of their knowledge of and expertise in the industry they are teaching about. In a teaching department, this usually results in a shared industry language and understanding. A shared industry language can help form a foundation for fostering a sense of solidarity.

Interestingly, in my research, I found that more experienced teachers had a broad understanding of what their industry was (for instance, the broader beauty therapy industry), whereas less experienced teachers sometimes had a narrower conceptualisation of their industry (for instance make-up or cosmetics). This can be a constraint for new teacher learning because new teachers were more willing to take teaching advice from other teachers who they considered to be part of their industry and less willing to take teaching advice from teachers outside their industry, regardless of those other teachers' teaching expertise (Francisco, 2017). It is useful to be mindful that new teachers, and some casually employed teachers that you are working with, may have a narrower view of what their "industry" is and may not feel that experienced teachers with a background in other sections of the industry have the understanding to be able to provide relevant teaching-related advice. Of course, this is not the case with all new teachers, and even less so with casually employed teachers who have been teaching for some time. It is, however, something to consider.

Training and education language

Many teachers come to VET and Further Education with a limited understanding of pedagogy/andragogy/teaching/training (hereafter referred to as teaching). In Australia and some other countries, this language also includes the language associated with competencies and training packages. New teachers are often still learning basic language and concepts related to teaching. In research I undertook with novice teachers, the teachers learnt this language at different rates and this was usually influenced by how often they were exposed to interactions with experienced teachers. A further constraint to learning became apparent in one of my research projects when one casually employed teacher who had limited opportunities to interact with experienced teachers had still not become familiar with teaching language after being employed for six months. The experienced teachers assumed she had this knowledge and she was too embarrassed to seek clarification. This resulted in some mistakes that affected student learning. Depending on how often the teachers interact with experienced teachers, the learning of teaching language can take quite some time. Some participants in my research never learnt the basic VET language even though they had undertaken the required Training and Assessment course within their first year of teaching. Learning teaching-related language was much better supported when there were opportunities to use it together with experienced teachers.

Material-economic arrangements

Material-economic arrangements influence the "doings" in a site. They can be the most extensive, or at least the most readily apparent, of the practice architectures that affect teacher learning. Examples are outlined below. It is important to remember that material-economic arrangements are usually entwined with cultural-discursive and social-political arrangements in affecting teacher learning. In VET and FE, important material-economic arrangements that influence teacher learning are usually physical arrangements, resources, and scheduling. However, the thing that has the most influence on teacher learning is teacher employment arrangements. The discussion begins with employment arrangements, and then goes on to address the other material-economic arrangements.

Teacher employment arrangements

We have known for some time that employment arrangements influence the practice architectures that teachers encounter. Seddon and Palmieri (2009) note:

> The fact that teachers enter an employment contract...means that they experience certain kinds of relationships with colleagues, clients,

associate professionals, and managers; organisational imperatives and ways of working in the workforce; and patterns of conflict and negotiation in workplace and industrial relations. Power and authority are important features of these experiences.

(p. 464)

Teacher employment arrangements are included here in the material-economic arrangements section, but, as the quote above suggests, they also extend into the social-political arrangements.

In my research into VET teacher learning, I have found that one of the key material-economic arrangements impacted by employment arrangements is where teachers are physically located in the workplace. Those teachers who are employed on a permanent basis, or on a long-term contract, are almost always physically co-located in the same staffroom area as other permanent/contract teachers. Those who are employed on a casual basis are usually located away from the permanent/contract teachers. This affects their access to support and advice from other teachers and the development of collegiality. As Boud and Hager (2012) note, a "lack of peers or lack of opportunities to participate with them…severely restricts opportunities and therefore development" (p. 26). Physical exclusion can also result in social exclusion, limiting teacher access to their colleagues.

Access to more structured professional development is another material-economic arrangement that is usually limited for casually employed teachers (Francisco, 2008; Guthrie, 2010). Guthrie argues that this limited access to both "ongoing support from other VET staff and to professional development opportunities" (p. 10) is concerning. Rainbird et al. (2004) note:

Patterns of inclusion and exclusion in workgroups, and the ability to move into related areas of work affect the capacity of workers to access informal learning. At the same time, entitlement to formal training and the capacity to access informal learning are also factors constitutive of the balance of power in the workplace.

(p. 40)

Inclusion and exclusion are discussed further in the *Social-political arrangements* section.

The rate of staff turnover is another material-economic arrangement that affects teacher learning. There are several issues related to a high staff turnover rate. For the organisation, staff turnover can be costly for many reasons including the cost of initial training, and administrative costs of bringing in new people. There is also the personal and professional cost to the teachers involved. The support of experienced VET and FE teachers is crucial for workplace learning (Francisco, 2017). These teachers are often expected to support the learning of new teachers on a voluntary basis (sometimes referred to as volunteerism). Staff turnover results in an increased workload for experienced teachers who support the new teachers. This can lead to experienced teachers becoming unwilling and/or unable to continue to volunteer to support the learning when there is an ongoing turnover of teachers. This is discussed further in the *Volunteerism* section below.

Physical arrangements

Physical arrangements relate to the physical items in a site that you can see. For instance, in a classroom this might include desks, chairs, and electronic whiteboards, as well as how they are arranged in relation to each other. In a staffroom, physical arrangements might include teachers' desks and computers (their workstations), as well as how the workstations are arranged in relation to each other. Physical arrangements also include things such as: the distance between staffrooms and teaching rooms, access (or lack thereof) to a staff tearoom/lunchroom, as well as how the tables and chairs in the tearoom/lunchroom are arranged. Other physical arrangements might include things such as access to a specially designed hair salon for teaching purposes (for Hairdressing teachers), or access to a specially designed gym for teaching purposes (for Sport and fitness teachers), and all the associated arrangements in these areas. Note, the practice architectures of a hairdressing salon or a gym that are designed for teaching purposes will be quite different to those in other areas of the teaching department.

Resources

In VET and FE, resources that can affect teacher learning include access to items such as well-developed quality lesson plans, subject outlines, assessment tasks, student handouts, and workbooks. Having access to high quality, well-designed teaching resources – especially for novice teachers – provides several benefits: for new teachers they provide examples of what is expected; they can be used immediately with little or no change to support student learning; and, importantly, they become a model for any future resources developed. Poor quality teaching resources provided to novice teachers are not just a limitation in the short term but can have long-term consequences as they inform teacher expectations for the development of future resources.

The availability of non-teaching staff can also influence teacher learning. Access to skilled administrative and technical staff can decrease the non-teaching-related time demands on teachers and help them successfully interact with, often bureaucratic, systems. In one site where I undertook research, the removal of the administrative officer resulted in teachers having to undertake the administrative work themselves (with no alteration to their teaching workload) in a system that was unfamiliar to them and that they found cumbersome, difficult to use, and time consuming. Time used for undertaking this work resulted in decreased time for teaching-related work. One teacher referred to the broader system in her organisation as "galumphing". Not only does access to administrative and technical staff result in more time available for teaching-related work and learning, often these staff are able to support teacher learning. One teacher noted:

> I really regard [Diane] as a valuable source of information…to have someone who knows the system that well, knows the students that well, you know, if I look back on my time and I think how have I got through all this, I would have to include [Diane] in that process.

Industry-related resources, such as access to appropriate products and resources for teaching, can also be valuable. In one of my research projects, I found that teachers were bringing their own industry relevant products (such as cosmetics) for student use because they were not provided by the college, or because the teacher did not know how to access what the college provided. At another site, teachers were asked to bring their own trade-related non-consumable resources from home.

Another important material-economic arrangement that can affect teacher learning is access to team teaching. Billett and Choy (2013) argue that most learning in the workplace takes place through "observation, mimesis (i.e. imitation) and practice" (p. 267). Team teaching gives teachers, especially new teachers, access to all three of these. In my research with novice VET teachers, I found that in each case where team teaching was available it was also combined with support and advice from the more experienced teacher, and it always supported teacher learning. The value of team teaching is not confined to novice teachers. Given the right conditions, all teachers can benefit from team teaching and the associated collegial discussions before and after teaching. In those organisations where arrangements can be made to enable it, the availability of team teaching is a material-economic arrangement that can be a powerful support for teacher learning.

Scheduling

In this section, we look at two scheduling-related issues – the scheduling of teaching hours, and the scheduling of a shared break. Experienced teachers who are employed permanently or on a long-term contract usually can choose when to undertake their teaching activities, and this is normally during the day. This often results in novice and casually employed teachers being scheduled to teach in the evenings. Such scheduling can result in these teachers having limited access to collegial interaction with, and advice from, the more experienced teachers, which can limit their learning.

The scheduling of a daily shared coffee break can be valuable in allowing teachers to interact in a relaxed atmosphere with their colleagues. The value of this (and associated arrangements such as a tearoom and communal table) in supporting teacher learning is discussed in more detail in Chapter 7.

Social-political arrangements

The social-political arrangements influence the "relatings" in a site. When people deliberately pay attention to creating a workplace that supports learning it is often the material-economic arrangements that are the focus. These can be the most apparent, and the most readily altered. It is important to be aware of the powerful influence that social-political arrangements can have on learning in the workplace. Dall'Alba (2009) argues:

> The process of becoming a professional occurs ... through continual interaction with other professionals, as well as those outside the professions. It is misleading to attempt to separate the individual from engagement with others in this process of becoming.
>
> (p. 42)

Workplace arrangements

Similarly, in relation to novice teachers, McNally et al. (2009) note that "the relational nature of beginning teachers' development is ... more than just a means or a context in which professional learning takes place; it is integral to becoming a teacher" (p. 326).

The theory of practice architectures identifies power and solidarity as important factors that enable and constrain practices. Issues of power and solidarity can include relationships of inclusion and exclusion. This can manifest in language (see Vignette 4.1), in physical arrangements as is often the case when casual teachers are placed in separate areas to permanently employed teachers, and in relationships (see Vignette 4.4). Trust is also an important aspect of social-political arrangements (trust is discussed further in Chapter 7).

Power and solidarity

The workplace is not always a harmonious environment. There inevitably will be differences and tensions. When tensions and disagreements occur within an environment where there is a sense of solidarity and trust, it is likely that people are willing to consider alternative approaches and views. This can be productive for ongoing development and innovation. However, where disagreements occur in environments of suspicion, surveillance, and distrust, it can be damaging for people, for productivity, and for achieving positive outcomes.

Issues of power will exist anywhere that people work or interact. Often when we think about power in the workplace, negative connotations surface, such as those associated with exploitation, surveillance, coercion, or manipulation. However, power can be much more than this, and can also be used in a positive and productive way. Smeed et al. (2009) highlight three different types of power that they argue are on a continuum: power over, power through, and power with.

Power over

The notion of 'power over' relates to the use of power for domination and control. It is often connected with an authoritarian approach by those who hold positional power. There are various ways that arrangements that enable 'power over' can influence the workplace. Some of these can be blatant and relatively easy to identify. Others can be more subtle. A 'power over' approach is likely to have negative outcomes. For instance, in one of the case studies examined by Francisco et al. (2021), a 'power over' approach resulted in silencing teachers, restricting teacher agency, and limiting teacher contributions to the project they were required to work on. The result included not only poor outcomes for the project, but also further decreased trust in the leader.

Power through

Power through involves the use of power (such as that created through position or knowledge) to facilitate positive outcomes for others. Two key features are negotiation and cooperation (Smeed et al., 2009, p. 35). This might include arrangements such as ensuring the availability of resources or scheduling that supports teaching learning (see Vignette 4.1) or arranging for teachers to team teach with an experienced teacher (see Vignettes 4.1 and 4.2).

Power with

'Power with' is a relational power and the key features are collegiality, connection, and trust (Smeed et al., 2009). A collaborative approach based on open communication is the hallmark of the use of 'power with'.

Volunteerism

The support of colleagues is an important component of teacher learning, especially for new teachers. The availability of this support is largely dependent on the volunteerism and goodwill of experienced teachers. Teacher workload affects their learning and capacity to support the learning of others (Davis, 2012). The workload of experienced teachers not only impacts their own learning, but it also impacts the learning of new teachers in their department. Harris et al. (2005) argue that an already heavy workload for experienced teachers is added to as a result of pressure to support the learning of new staff. They note:

> Experienced staff are obliged to spend considerable time explaining new delivery systems and accountability requirements. Additional tasks such as these create significant amounts of 'incidental' work for the shrinking core of permanent staff.
>
> (p. 66)

Workplace arrangements

In my research, I have found that when experienced teachers were overloaded, they were less likely to voluntarily support new teachers, and new teachers were less likely to seek their support.

As noted earlier, the theory of practice architectures has been introduced to allow us to consider how different arrangements in the workplace enable and constrain teacher learning. Next, we consider what this looks like in reality, through the stories of real teachers.

Practice architectures that enable and constrain teacher learning in the workplace

Practice architectures that enable and constrain teacher learning vary from site to site (Francisco, 2020a). Even where a similar arrangement is available, the interaction with other arrangements might result in support for teacher learning in one site and not in another. It is therefore not possible to claim that certain practice architectures will always support teacher learning in the workplace, or will always constrain teacher learning. When working to support teacher learning in our own local site, what we can do is trial those arrangements that have supported teacher learning in other sites, to determine if they are effective in our own site. The vignettes below outline arrangements that have enabled and constrained teacher learning.

Vignette 4.1 outlines the practice architectures that enabled and constrained Ewan's learning in the Air Conditioning and Refrigeration Department. These practice architectures are outlined separately but, in reality, they are inter-related.

Vignette 4.1 Air Conditioning and Refrigeration – Ewan

Ewan joined the Air Conditioning and Refrigeration Department as a teacher after operating his own air conditioning and refrigeration business for some years. Below are the practice architectures that he encountered in his first 18 months of teaching.

Cultural-discursive arrangements

The language of the air conditioning and refrigeration trade was used when teaching and chatting with colleagues. As a result of the material-economic arrangements (see below), the language of the electrical industry was also used.

The language of vocational education and training (VET) was regularly used. For various reasons, including being immersed in the language, Ewan picked up VET language relatively quickly compared with some of the teachers in other departments who started at the same time as him. Interestingly, in this site, the language of VET was valued, but this was seen as quite different to the language of school education. Teaching approaches that were not accepted by many of the teachers, such as yelling at students, were referred to as being from the schoolroom. One teacher who did this and who was also considered to be unreasonably inflexible with students, was referred to as a 'school master' in a pejorative way. A large proportion of the air conditioning and refrigeration teachers had a Bachelor of Adult Education teaching qualification, and an even larger proportion of the Electrical teachers had this degree. (This was unusual in the organisation more broadly, and a source of pride within the department.) This affected the language used and concepts discussed.

Often as I walked into the tearoom or staffroom, the call would go out 'Ducks on the pond', which I later discovered was a warning that women were present and language needed to be regulated. When women were present (except for one Electrical teacher, see social-political arrangements below) swearing and vulgar language was not used.

When Ewan began as a teacher in the Air Conditioning and Refrigeration Department, he already shared the industry language. Through his mentor, and the shared discussions across the desks and in the tearoom (see material-economic arrangements), Ewan was stirred into the language of the department. Ewan also undertook a certificate level teaching qualification during his first semester of teaching. This qualification explicitly used VET language and supported teachers to understand relevant concepts. Ewan's ongoing discussions with his mentor and colleagues further supported his learning of relevant language and concepts.

Material-economic arrangements

Several material-economic arrangements supported teacher learning, including physical arrangements, scheduling, and access to resources. The Air Conditioning and Refrigeration staffroom was open-plan, with teachers easily able to see each other and chat across their desks. The teachers shared a long rectangular staffroom with the Electrical Department, with one department at either end of the room. The Electrical teachers had chosen to set up their desks as separate workstations, whereas the Air Conditioning and Refrigeration Department had chosen to have all desks together with teachers beside and across from each other, and no partitions. Ewan identified the ongoing cross-desk chat as something that supported his learning.

The Air Conditioning and Refrigeration Department shared a tearoom/lunchroom with the Electrical Department. The tearoom had a large communal table as well as boiling water, a sink and a refrigerator. Scheduling arrangements that enabled a daily shared morning tea (referred to as 'smoko') from 10.00–10.30 had been established for many years. This enabled valuable discussions that supported teacher learning (discussed in more detail in Chapter 7).

There was a low staff turnover in the Air Conditioning and Refrigeration Department and most of the teachers were experienced and highly skilled. The department did not often have new teachers, and experienced teachers were not overwhelmed by the needs of novice and inexperienced teachers (discussed further below in the social-political section).

Support staff also formed part of the material-economic arrangements of the department. The Air Conditioning and Refrigeration Department had an experienced technical support officer and an experienced administration officer. Having this work undertaken by people specialising in these tasks (unlike some of the other teaching departments in the same organisation) meant that teachers did not need to add these tasks (and the associated time demands, and learning required) to their workload. The Head of School had been working in the role for many years and had developed strong relationships throughout the organisation. He knew how things operated, both officially and unofficially, and was able to ensure the department had good access to resources. The department also had good access to physical resources for teaching purposes, including both consumables and equipment (this can be understood as an example of the use of 'power through').

While the organisation more broadly did not allow for team teaching (payment arrangements and staff scheduling only allowed for one teacher to be paid for each scheduled class, and the administration system could not accommodate team teaching arrangements), the experienced Head of School had made arrangements so that team teaching was possible to support the learning of new teachers (another example of 'power through'). For each new subject that Ewan was to teach, his mentor established a team-teaching arrangement with someone who had previously taught the subject (often the mentor himself). Ewan found this to be beneficial to his learning. Team teaching meant that Ewan had access to feedback from an experienced teacher based on observations during teaching, the opportunity to observe the teaching approach of an experienced teacher, well-developed resources, co-creation of new resources, debriefing after each teaching session, as well as critical reflection together with the experienced teacher.

Social-political arrangements

The material-economic arrangements supported the development of social-political arrangements in the Air Conditioning and Refrigeration Department enabling teacher learning. In relation to all matters associated with being a teacher (including teaching, resource development, assessment development, and pastoral care for students) the teachers supported each other's ongoing learning and development. Ewan noted:

> It's just a constant conversation we've been having and we go through it that way.

The conversation took place not only in meetings that were deliberately set up to review and work on assessment tasks, resource development, and teaching approaches, but also continued across the desks and at smoko.

The language use discussed above was exclusionary for various groups – those unfamiliar with the language of the trade, those unfamiliar with VET language, and those unfamiliar with more academic education language. As alluded to in relation to cultural-discursive arrangements, the workplace (like the industry) was male dominated and women were also excluded from some discussions. One of the Electrical teachers was a woman, and she was in many ways understood as an 'honorary male'. (It is not the work of this book to address gender issues; however, it is worth noting that an understanding of the theory of practice architectures can also allow deeper analysis in this area.) These shared languages that excluded outsiders also served to create inclusion and a sense of solidarity within the teaching team.

The Air Conditioning and Refrigeration Department was made up of a strong team of experienced teachers who supported each other's learning. This often resulted in a high level of volunteerism, especially for one long-term teacher (who was Ewan's mentor and who had mentored most of the other teachers in the department at some time). The relatively low staff turnover in this department meant that when teachers were volunteering their time and energy to support the learning of others, they could also see it as investing in the long-term development of a collegial team.

The next vignette, set on a different campus and in a different teaching area, illustrates some similar and some quite different practice architectures.

Vignette 4.2 Year 1 – Community Services Department – Alice

Cultural-discursive arrangements

The Community Services Department had a shared language related to the community services and community development industries. The teachers all spoke this 'industry' language and they were supporting their students to learn it. This was entwined with a valuing of their students who were either working in the community services industry or preparing to do so. Alice articulated the shared language and values in the following way:

"I like the people that I'm working with. They are my kind of people ... their understanding of their subject matter is extremely advanced. And I find it very interesting to talk to them about, you know ... we're on the same page as far as professional, and even some life interests. So, my kind of people!"

VET language was regularly used within the department. Alice interacted with experienced teachers daily and picked this language up relatively quickly.

Material-economic arrangements

The Community Services staffroom was a long rectangle with workstations either side of the rectangle, and a wide aisle up the middle. Each teacher had a separate workstation, and these were separated from each other by a partition. There was relatively little interaction across the workstations. However, another physical arrangement, a large communal table, was conducive to teacher interaction and was used regularly. (This is discussed in more detail in Chapter 7.)

There were various resources that supported Alice's learning. When asked to teach a new subject, Alice was provided with well-developed assessment tasks, lesson plans and subject guides. The Community Services Department also had a tradition of using workbooks comprising case studies and associated questions and tasks. The case studies were usually developed from news stories. In addition to using these workbooks with her students, Alice also found they supported her own knowledge of the depth of understanding students were expected to develop. From early in her teaching, Alice added more case studies for use in her own classes and for the use of other teachers.

Although considered a 'public provider' of VET education, the college where Alice was employed encouraged each department to develop commercial arrangements with individual businesses to supplement their income (or lack thereof). The Community Services

Department had a tradition of being innovative in their teaching, and of working together with industry organisations to develop training courses to meet the needs of the organisation. Alice was initially employed on a casual basis. Due to exceptional circumstances, including the health of some experienced teachers, after three weeks she was given responsibility for delivery of an entire qualification for one of these commercial arrangements. She found this daunting and felt she did not have sufficient knowledge and skills to undertake this work. Alice noted:

> I just struggled with the whole…the format of it, the set-up…I think I'm too new to have really got in there and I felt very little control of the process. All in all, I found it very stressful.

While very stressful (and not a recommended approach), the social-political arrangements (see below) pushed Alice to learn rapidly. Throughout the two years that Alice was a participant in the research project, she undertook a number of these commercial projects. Each of the sites had different practice architectures to the campus and to each other. Developing a familiarity with these practice architectures and working to support the learning of students in a range of different sites (while being mentored by experienced teachers) was an important aspect of Alice's learning.

The Community Services Department had a low staff turnover. Most of the teachers had been teaching in the department for many years and it was relatively rare for a new teacher to be employed. Casually employed teachers were given workstations in the same area as the experienced teachers (in the various research projects I have been involved with I have found this to be relatively rare), and had access to ad hoc advice and support.

Social-political arrangements

The Community Services Department had a strong ethos of respect for colleagues and students, and this formed a solid basis for the social-political arrangements in the department. Alice noted:

> I felt supported, emotionally, by the fact that they're pleasant people to be with, and that's been a really nourishing, supportive factor. There is a nice sort of vibe there, and people are good to each other, and share resources.
>
> It is likely that the social-political arrangements were influenced by the low staff turnover. Unlike some other teaching departments, experienced teachers were only rarely called upon to support new teachers. They could also have relatively high expectations that any new teachers would remain for some time, and the initial support provided was likely to result in the development of a competent long-term team member.
>
> Alice was well supported by two separate mentors (each focussing on a different area of teaching). This included providing her with resources, debriefing after classes, reflecting together, working with her on resource development, and sometimes team teaching with her. Alice found this particularly valuable when she was teaching on the commercial projects because it not only supported her learning, but it also reduced her sense of isolation. The mentoring and team teaching also supported the development of a closer relationship with each of these teachers.

By the end of her first year of teaching, Alice had learnt a lot, and had taken on a number of difficult teaching projects (including the commercial projects discussed above). Everything she was given to do she did professionally and successfully. She was thriving as a teacher and was highly respected and valued within her teaching department.

In her second year of teaching, the practice architectures changed.

Vignette 4.3 Year 2 – Community Services Department/Online Learning Department – Alice

After about a year of teaching, Alice was asked to develop an entire qualification to be taught online. Most of her week was devoted to this new project, with some additional teaching on commercial projects.

Cultural-discursive arrangements

The cultural-discursive arrangements included language related to online learning, which was new to Alice. The language of the community services industry, which had been a point of connection with the community services teachers, was not used. Similarly, the language of classroom or other face-to-face teaching, which Alice had become proficient in, was also not used. The online learning language was foreign to her, she had limited access to it in day-to-day conversations, and she found it difficult to learn. After working on development of the online qualification for some months, Alice noted:

> I realised I hadn't actually learnt a lot of the things I needed to have learnt. They just didn't stick in my brain.

Alice's limited understanding of the online learning language, and practice architectures that constrained her in developing her understanding of the language and online learning more broadly, was further exacerbated by her being dubious about whether online education was the appropriate medium for community services workers who needed to have well-developed personal and communication skills. This belief was also held by many of the community services teachers she worked with.

> It's not just me, the rest of the people in my team either don't use it at all, or can only really use ... [Jenny] can use it a bit, and [Mike] can use it a bit, the others don't even want to go near it. They hate it, they find it ... it's not inviting to them, they haven't got the time to do stuff on it ... it's like an imposition and a resentment.

The cultural-discursive arrangements of language limitations, further exacerbated by her community services colleagues' lack of valuing of online learning (which reinforced her own concerns), limited Alice's learning. It is interesting to consider this in relation to her rapid learning of VET language and broader education related language when she first began as a teacher.

Material-economic arrangements

When she began working on developing the online qualification, Alice was given a new workstation in the Online Learning Department, which was located in a different part of the campus to the Community Services Department. Given the lack of valuing of online learning among the community services teachers, and the value of learning from incidental interactions with colleagues, this move to the Online Learning Department had the potential to support Alice's learning: a potential that was not fulfilled due to some constraining practice architectures.

The Online Learning Department was in a long rectangular room with workstations either side of the aisle. This is where the similarity to the Community Services staffroom ends. As a 'visitor' to the department, Alice's workstation was separated from everyone else by a brick wall. There was no chance to overhear discussions, no easy way to ask ad hoc questions, and no communal table where teachers gathered for tea breaks or to work together. For Alice to engage with anyone from the Online Learning Department, she had to walk to the aisle in front of the person's workstation and have any discussions standing in the aisle.

The small Online Learning Department was expected to support online learning development across a large organisation. They had made the decision some time before Alice's arrival that one-to-one support for individual teachers was not viable with their limited staff numbers and the high demands of the organisation. As a result of a favour to the Head of Faculty, the head of the Online Learning Department (Pamela) was identified as Alice's mentor for the development of the online qualification. The social-political impact of these material-economic arrangements is discussed further in the section on next page.

Workplace arrangements

Social-political arrangements

Alice found it difficult to engage with people from the Online Learning Department. Her previously successful approaches in the Community Services Department, such as having a chat at the communal table, or having regular ad hoc meetings with her mentors were not available to her in this new environment. There was no space where she could engage with the online learning teachers in a personal or more relaxed way (such as was possible at the communal table in the Community Services Department – see Chapter 7). The decision taken by the Online Learning Department, some time before Alice's arrival, not to support teachers one-to-one meant that people resisted answering any ad hoc questions that she had. The mentor that she was given, limited their meetings to an hour once a week, which Alice found difficult. Alice and the online learning team had different expectations about how Alice would learn to develop the qualification that she was to put online. Alice had expected that her learning would be supported through ongoing interactions with online learning staff. The online learning team expected Alice to develop her skills and understanding largely through reading 'how to' documents, undertaking short courses, and 'trial and error'. As a result of these different expectations, Alice's relationship with the online learning team was at times strained. She noted:

> A lot of lovely people had been helping me, some of them getting a bit impatient with my slowness and doing things for me…But now I [have lost all the work that I had done]. I've got to go back and do it all again, basically, which is probably quite good, because I think I'd do it slightly differently now.

After 'losing' the work that she had done for the online qualification in the first four months, Alice enrolled in an online learning course. Alice's motivation, confidence and sense of achievement from her successes in the previous year were no longer evident.

> I've enrolled myself in the advanced [Online Learning] course which I'm doing now, to really address my own deficiencies.

By the end of the research project and the end of Alice's second year of teaching, the online qualification still had not been developed.

So what?

No-one had deliberately worked to constrain Alice's learning; however, decisions made for other purposes had resulted in quite strong constraints. The clever, motivated, confident, fast learning, high achiever from the first year became unsure of her capabilities, unmotivated and unable to move forward with her project.

Often when teachers fail to thrive in the workplace, the focus is on the perceived deficiencies of the individual teacher. Alice's experience shows the powerful impact that practice architectures can have in enabling and constraining teacher learning.

It is sometimes assumed that an organisation will have similar practice architectures in each local site. This is not the case – each site within an organisation will differ. In this book, in most cases we are considering the boundaries of a local site to be an entire teaching department; although there are some examples where the boundaries are much smaller than this, especially when a teaching department is separated physically into several locations. The vignette below, focussing on online learning, illustrates the importance of looking at each site individually rather than at an organisation more broadly to determine the practice architectures that enable and constrain particular practices.

Vignette 4.4 Online Learning – Simon

In the large VET organisation where Simon was employed as a teacher, there was strong support for online learning. This included funding, training and equipment. The organisation was considered to be innovative and to have a well-established online learning approach.

In his first year of teaching, Simon was introduced to online learning through the Certificate IV in Training and Assessment that he was undertaking. The teachers of that qualification encouraged him

Workplace arrangements

to use the online learning platform to provide a blended learning approach for his students. Additionally, he had a mentor (from another teaching department) who was valued throughout the organisation for her online learning skills and who supported many teachers across her faculty to undertake online learning.

Simon worked in the Electronics department. In his first year of teaching, he tried to introduce several new approaches to the department. These approaches, including offering blended learning for all students, were consistent with expectations within the broader organisation. However, in Simon's department there was no interest in, and even resistance to, new approaches including the use of online or blended learning. Simon, with the support of his mentor, worked to offer a blended approach for his students that allowed those who missed face-to-face classes (due to employer requirements or illness) to access learning materials online. This was also of value for all students in allowing them to revisit information that had been presented in class.

There were a number of practice architectures that constrained a blended learning approach. Simon's department did not have access to teaching rooms with an electronic whiteboard when he began as a teacher; however, with the support of his mentor he was able to arrange access to a room that was about 800 metres away from the usual teaching rooms (which also held the practical equipment that was used in many of the classes). Simon's classes were therefore split between two classrooms with the first part of the class in the new teaching room, and the second part in the 'usual' teaching room where students could access equipment for the practical component of the lesson. To access a laptop and overhead projector Simon needed to borrow one from the library (which was even further from the new teaching room) and carry them to and from the new room each lesson. This became quite a burden to arrange each week. Also, as noted, Simon's colleagues were not supportive of a blended learning approach. After trying to introduce a few new approaches, Simon was counselled by his supervisor not to make too many waves. He noted:

> I've had to step back and say OK ... I can't push it. I don't feel like I can push it anymore, because I pushed a little bit on a

> few different ideas, and ... I've come in from industry and the first few months I think I pushed pretty hard on 'why are we doing it this way?' And 'why [are there such poor graduation outcomes]? And 'maybe we're doing something wrong', but it wasn't received very well. So, I've got to step back and say 'well maybe I come across as arrogant' ... nobody likes to feel they're being told that [what they're doing is wrong]. So, just waiting.

Simon thus realised that any changes he made would have to be slowly introduced. Lest you assume that Simon was a difficult character and was in fact arrogant (as he suggests above), in my interviews and monthly emails with Simon over the two years of the research project, I found no evidence of this. Instead, I found him to be amiable, communicative, reflective and intelligent, with a strong focus on doing the best he could to support the learning of his students. Not only were the changes that Simon was suggesting and modelling consistent with expectations within the organisation more broadly, they were also consistent with the requirements of the curriculum, and of the industry. However, they were inconsistent with the traditions of his teaching department and by challenging these approaches, his relationships with his colleagues deteriorated. This also resulted in a decreased willingness of experienced teachers to support Simon's learning in other areas. In discussing the lack of support available to him, he noted:

> "My biggest challenge is ... staying positive in an environment where I feel a lack of support, not becoming too focussed on the negatives...not getting frustrated with the system, but just focussing on the teaching. That's my biggest challenge.

Without the support of his supervisor or the teaching team, Simon was unable to sustain the changes that he tried to implement. By the end of his first year of teaching, he was no longer offering a blended learning approach for his students.

Simon's experience is consistent with McNally et al.'s (2009) finding that, "It is a feeling of being supported, rather than the acquisition of specified bits of professional knowledge, that seems to matter most" (p. 326).

Workplace arrangements

In addition to other practice architectures, this lack of support affected Simon's learning, his experience of being a teacher, and his way of teaching.

Individual agency

So far, this chapter has shown the powerful impact that the practice architectures in a site can have in enabling and constraining teacher learning in the workplace. As noted at the beginning of this chapter, the practice architectures present or brought into a site prefigure, but do not predetermine, the actions and practices that individual teachers, or groups of teachers, undertake. Vignette 4.4 is a clear illustration of this. However, individuals can, and do, make a difference (see Chapter 8). Vignette 4.5 below provides an example of change made by the actions of one individual.

Vignette 4.5 Individual agency – Sam

When Sam joined the Building Design teaching department, he had a strong focus on being available for his two young children after school and supporting his wife in her career. Before Sam joined the department there was a history of teachers spending long hours on campus. Sam's other obligations and priorities did not allow for this and he arranged to do a lot of his non-teaching work at home so that he could pick his children up from school. The employment of another (male) teacher who similarly limited his on-campus time led to a change in the actions of many teachers in the department so that having extended hours on campus became the exception rather than the norm.

So What?

The change to the number of hours spent on campus of many of the teachers could be seen as a relatively minor change, especially as it is unlikely that it resulted in a decrease in the total number of hours worked. Also, Sam's goal was not to change the practices of all teachers but to instead ensure he could be at home for his family. However, it provides evidence of how an individual can change practices. It is

> likely that Sam's gender and his profession (he was still undertaking some architecture work in addition to his teaching role) affected his power to be able to do this. Nonetheless, Sam's agency served to change the practices in the department.

Individuals will interact with existing practice architectures in various ways depending on their own dispositions, priorities, prior experiences and motivations (Kemmis et al., 2017). As Kemmis et al. note, "We make our worlds by acting within them, but we do so in ways that are constrained" (p. 249). Vignette 4.6 below provides another illustration of individual agency resulting in change.

Vignette 4.6 Individual agency – Tamsin

Tamsin is a Foundation Studies teacher at a relatively small VET college in a regional area (Regional Campus). Before taking up the role at Regional Campus she was a teacher in a VET college in her hometown (Hometown Campus). Regional Campus is about an hour from Hometown Campus and both colleges are part of a large state-wide VET organisation.

When Tamsin started teaching at Regional Campus, she discovered that the computer resources available for her Foundation Studies students were very limited and she could not access further resources through the usual channels. Tamsin's students were rarely computer literate and did not own their own computers. Once the students completed Foundation Studies, future training possibilities were almost entirely online. Tamsin thus saw the lack of computer facilities as a real barrier for them moving forward. Through engaging with the IT department at Hometown Campus and developing a good relationship with the staff, Tamsin was able to learn to fix existing computers on Regional Campus, access other computers for student use, and gain a better understanding of how to support the computer literacy and computer access for her students. Through her own agency, Tamsin could access support for her own learning, which resulted in supporting the learning of her students. This is discussed in more detail in Chapter 7.

The two vignettes focussing on individual agency show teachers acting on their own to make changes. Chapter 8 focusses on changes that leaders and groups of teachers can make.

Concluding comments

As noted earlier in this chapter, it is not possible to claim that particular practice architectures will always enable or constrain teacher learning. However, we do know that the following practice architectures in, or brought into, a site tend to be good enablers of teacher learning in the teaching workplace: a shared industry language; a shared language related to VET and teaching; co-located workstations; a regularly used communal table; team teaching; pre-existing quality resources such as lesson plans and assessment tasks that can also be a model for the future development of resources; mentoring; opportunities for observing other teachers; opportunities to be observed by other teachers and to receive supportive feedback; access to professional development; the support of colleagues and supervisors; a regularly scheduled morning tea; a collegial workplace; and inclusion in discussions and decision making.

There are also some arrangements that are likely to constrain teacher learning in the workplace, and many of these relate to a lack of enabling arrangements outlined in the paragraph above. In addition, exclusion can be a powerful constraint to teacher learning. Across the various research projects that I have been involved with, perhaps the most apparent and wide-ranging exclusion is of casual teachers, but as Vignettes 4.3 and 4.4 showed, it is not limited to casual teachers, and it is not always deliberate.

Questions to consider

These questions are relevant for this chapter as well as for Chapter 8. The survey suggestions provided in Chapter 8 will support you in addressing these questions.

For the individual

- Do a practice architectures survey of the site where you work. Even better if you can do this with a trusted colleague (or colleagues).
  - What cultural-discursive arrangements enable your learning?
  - What cultural-discursive arrangements constrain your learning?

- What cultural-discursive arrangements enable the learning of others (casual teachers, experienced teachers, novice teachers)?
- What cultural-discursive arrangements constrain the learning of others (casual teachers, experienced teachers, novice teachers)?
- Consider each of these four questions for material-economic and social-political arrangements.
- What changes might be made to better support your learning and the learning of your colleagues?
  - Who might support you in making these changes?

See Chapter 8 for more ideas.

For the organisation

- For each local site (probably each teaching department, but if a teaching department is in more than one site, it will need to be in each site) do a survey of the practice architectures that enable and constrain teacher learning. Consider:
  - What cultural-discursive arrangements enable teacher learning?
    - Explicitly consider each group – experienced teachers, novice teachers, casually employed teachers.
  - What cultural-discursive arrangements constrain teacher learning?
    - Explicitly consider each group – experienced teachers, novice teachers, casually employed teachers.
  - Be careful not to assume that two departments physically similar, or with other similarities have the same practice architectures.
  - If possible, engage the teachers in each department to be involved in the survey.
- After the survey, consider what changes can be made to further enable teacher learning in the workplace in relation to the cultural-discursive, material-economic and social-political dimensions. Identify changes for the:
  - Short term (in the next week)
  - Medium term (in the next 6 months)
  - Longer term (in the next 1–2 years)
- Consider who should be involved in the planning and implementation of these changes.

See Chapter 8 for more ideas.

Further reading

Kemmis, S., Wilkinson, J., Edwards-Groves, C., Grootenboer, P., Hardy, I., & Bristol, L. (2014). *Changing practices, changing education*. Singapore: Springer.

This was the first book that outlined the theory of practice architectures in detail.

Mahon, K., Kemmis, S., Francisco, S., & Lloyd, A. (2017). Introduction: practice theory and the theory of practice architectures. In K. Mahon, S. Francisco, & S. Kemmis (Eds.), *Exploring education and professional practice: through the lens of practice architectures*. Singapore: Springer.

This chapter provides a summary of the theory of practice architectures.

For further reading where the theory of practice architectures is used to analyse VET teacher learning in the workplace, see my 2017 and 2020 articles in the reference list below.

References

Billett, S., & Choy, S. (2013). Learning through work: emerging perspectives and new challenges. *Journal of Workplace Learning*, 25(4), 264–276.

Boud, D., & Hager, P. (2012). Re-thinking continuing professional development through changing metaphors and location in professional practices. *Studies in Continuing Education*, 34(1), 17–30. doi:10.1080/0158037X.2011.608656

Dall'Alba. (2009). Learning professional ways of being: ambiguities of becoming. *Educational Philosophy and Theory*, 41(1), 34–45. doi:10.1111/j.1469-5812.2008.00475.x

Davis, C. (2012). Practice as complexity: encounters with management education in the public sector. In P. Hager, A. Lee, & A. Reich (Eds.), *Practice, learning and change: practice-theory perspectives on professional learning*. Springer. doi:10.1007/978-94-007-4774-6

Eraut, M. (2004). Informal learning in the workplace. *Studies in Continuing Education*, 26(2), 247–273. doi:http://dx.doi.org/10.1080/158037042000225245

Francisco, S. (2020a). Developing a trellis of practices that support learning in the workplace. *Studies in Continuing Education*, 42(1), 102–117. https://doi.org/10.1080/0158037X.2018.1562439

Francisco, S. (2020b). What novice vocational education and training teachers learn in the teaching workplace. *International Journal of Training Research*, 18(1), 37–54. doi: 10.1080/14480220.2020.1747785

Francisco, S. (2017). Mentoring as part of a trellis of practices that support learning. In K. Mahon, S. Francisco, & S. Kemmis (Eds.), *Exploring education and professional practice: through the lens of practice architectures*. Singapore: Springer. doi:10.1007/978-981-10-2219-7

Francisco, S. (2008). Professional development: what casual TAFE teachers want, Australian Vocational Education and Training Research Association Conference, April 2008, Adelaide. Refereed conference paper. Retrieved from https://avetra.org.au/data/Conference_2008_pres./56._Susanne_Francisco.pdf

Francisco, S., Forssten Seiser, A., & Grice, C. (2021). Professional learning that enables the development of critical praxis. *Professional Development in Education*, 1–15. doi:10.1080/19415257.2021.1879228

Guthrie, H. (2010). Professional development in the vocational education and training workforce. Adelaide: NCVER. Retrieved from www.ncver.edu.au/research-and-statistics/publications/all-publications/professional-development-in-the-vocational-education-and-training-workforce

Harris, R., Simons, M., & Clayton, B. (2005). Shifting mindsets: the changing work roles of vocational education and training practitioners. Adelaide: NCVER. Retrieved from www.ncver.edu.au/publications/publications/all-publications/shifting-mindsets-the-changing-work-roles-of-vocational-education-and-training-practitioners

Kemmis, S., Wilkinson, J., & Edwards-Groves, C. (2017). Roads not Travelled, Roads Ahead: How the theory of practice architectures is travelling. In K. Mahon, S. Francisco, & S. Kemmis (Eds.), *Exploring education and professional practice: through the lens of practice architectures*. Singapore: Springer. doi:10.1007/978-981-10-2219-7

Kemmis, S., Wilkinson, J., Edwards-Groves, C., Grootenboer, P., Hardy, I., & Bristol, L. (2014). *Changing practices, changing education*. Singapore: Springer. doi:10.1007/978-981-4560-47-4

Lucas, N., & Unwin, L. (2009). Developing teacher expertise at work: in-service trainee teachers in colleges of further education in England. *Journal of Further and Higher Education*, *33*(4), 423–433. doi:10.1080/03098770903272503

Mahon, K., Kemmis, S., Francisco, S., & Lloyd, A. (2017). Introduction: practice theory and the theory of practice architectures. In K. Mahon, S. Francisco, & S. Kemmis (Eds.), *Exploring education and professional practice: through the lens of practice architectures*. Singapore: Springer. doi:10.1007/978-981-10-2219-7

McNally, J., Blake, A., & Reid, A. (2009). The informal learning of new teachers in school. *Journal of Workplace Learning*, *21*(4), 322–333. doi:10.1108/13665620910954210

Nicolini, D. (2012). *Practice theory, work, and organisation: an introduction*. Oxford: Oxford University Press.

Orr, K. (2019). VET teachers and trainers. In D. Guile & L. Unwin (Eds.), *The Wiley handbook of Vocational Education and Training*. Hoboken, NJ: Wiley & Sons. doi:10.1002/9781119098713

Rainbird, H., Munro, A., & Holly, L. (2004). The employment relationship and workplace learning. In H. Rainbird, A. Fuller, & A. Munro (Eds.), *Workplace learning in context*. London: Routledge. https://doi.org/10.4324/9780203571644

Seddon, T., & Palmieri, P. (2009). Teachers' work, power and authority. In L. Saha & A. G. Dworkin (Eds.), *International handbook of research on teachers and teaching* (pp. 463–479). New York, NY: Springer.

Smeed, J., Kimber, M., Millwater, J., & Ehrich, L. (2009). Power over, with and through: Another look at micropolitics. *Leading and Managing, 15*(1), 26–41.

A trellis of practices that support learning
More than mentoring

Previous chapters have discussed a range of practices that support teacher learning as well as the arrangements that enable and constrain teacher learning. This chapter outlines the concept of a trellis of practices that support learning (PSLs) (Francisco, 2017, 2020). Inter-related PSLs can form a sturdy structure (trellis) that can provide a strong support for teacher learning. The components of this structure vary, but it almost always includes mentoring. In this chapter, the concept of a trellis of PSLs is explained. The concept is illustrated through examples of real sites where teachers are working, beginning with a site where there was no trellis of inter-related practices, and ending with a well-developed trellis of PSLs.

Practices that support learning (PSLs)

When teachers learn in the workplace, they usually engage in several practices to support their learning. PSLs include some of the things that were outlined in Chapter 4, such as team teaching, using existing well-designed resources, reading, and so on. On their own, each of these individual PSLs are valuable in supporting learning. In the research that I undertook with Australian Vocational Education and Training (VET) teachers (Francisco, 2017), it became apparent that, when PSLs inter-relate with each other, teacher learning is more strongly supported. This is consistent with Husband's (2018) findings in research that he did with Further Education (FE) teachers in Scotland and Wales. Husband found that where learning practices "were linked the respondents recalled positive impacts to practice and where they were not linked or absent, negative impact was frequently recalled and had a lasting effect in practice" (p. 176).

DOI: 10.4324/9781003112624-5

The value of inter-relationships between PSLs is also consistent with the theory of ecologies of practices (Kemmis et al., 2012; Mahon et al., 2017), which is a sub-theory of the theory of practice architectures (Kemmis et al., 2014), which you encountered in Chapter 4. Using the theory of ecologies of practices, we can see that "practices, like biological systems, can form inter-related webs, and that one practice can form the practice architectures for another practice" (Francisco, 2017, p. 109). For the teachers in my studies, some of the practices that they undertook to support their learning became practice architectures that enhanced the outcomes of other practices that supported their learning.

A trellis of practices that support learning (PSLs)

We begin our illustration of the concept of a trellis of PSLs by telling Trevor's story.

Vignette 5.1 Trevor: no inter-related PSLs

As you may recall from Chapter 2, Trevor is a teacher who is employed at a large Technical and Further Education (TAFE) organisation. He was employed on a permanent basis straight from industry, with no experience of teaching and no teaching qualifications. At his job interview, he was told that there were a number of permanently employed teachers in the team, as well as a Head of School. When he started work a month or so later, all the permanent teachers had resigned, and the Head of School had been promoted to a higher-level position in another team and was not replaced. The remaining teachers in the team were all employed on a casual basis. There is a tradition of casually employed teachers in this department arriving just in time for teaching a class, and leaving immediately after.

While Trevor had been working in the industry for more than 30 years when he started as a teacher, much of what he was teaching was either entirely new to him, or was something that he had learnt decades previously. Trevor therefore needed to learn both the content of what he was teaching as well as all the things associated with being a teacher. To learn the content, Trevor uses a range of strategies including reading textbooks, reading the workbooks that are provided for students, and reading relevant manuals. To learn to teach, he mostly relies on trial and error, doing what his own teachers had done more than three decades ago, and making slight adjustments when students complain. Trevor has a mentor from another teaching department. However, the mentor is not familiar with Trevor's teaching area, and there is no clear interaction between the mentoring and the other practices that Trevor uses to support his learning, such as reading, watching the casual teachers teach, and undertaking formal study.

Contrast Trevor's experience with the experience that Sarah had.

Vignette 5.2 Sarah: limited inter-related PSLs

When Sarah began as a teacher, all the teaching she did involved team teaching with her mentor. Her mentor provides her with well-prepared resources and these form the basis of her teaching. Sarah also trials approaches and makes adjustments as appropriate (see Figure 5.1). This relatively simple inter-relationship between mentoring, team teaching, and access to well-prepared resources is of value in supporting Sarah's learning. Sarah also engages with other PSLs, including reading through teaching resources developed for Business Administration subjects that she had not formally studied, reading relevant textbooks, formal study of a Certificate IV in Training and Assessment, as well as formal study for a Business Administration qualification. None of these other PSLs are clearly inter-related with the four identified in Figure 5.1.

Trellis of practices that support learning

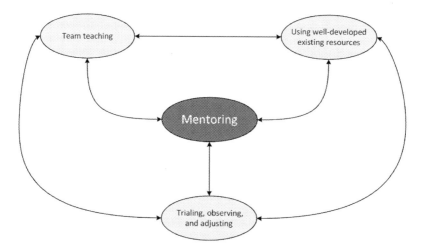

Figure 5.1 Sarah: limited inter-related PSLs

Next, we consider the PSLs for Sam in the Design Department.

> ## Vignette 5.3 Sam: the development of a trellis of PSLs
>
> Sam is employed in the Design Department where there has been quite a lot of thought given to supporting the ongoing development of teachers, including new teachers as well as those with more experience. Thinking back to the practice architectures discussed in Chapter 4, it is worth noting that the Head of School and Head of Faculty are experienced in these roles and have had some years to develop these supportive arrangements. Sam has access to several inter-related PSLs (see Figure 5.2). He has a mentor, who he also sometimes team teaches with. His mentor provides him with well-developed resources. She also works with Sam to collaboratively develop new resources. Co-teaching (where two teachers teach the same curriculum to two different cohorts of students in the same semester) occurs for some of the subjects Sam teaches, and Sam sometimes works together with a co-teacher to collaboratively develop new resources. Sam also has good access to his colleagues within the shared office space. He also trials different approaches, observes outcomes, and makes alterations as appropriate.

Trellis of practices that support learning

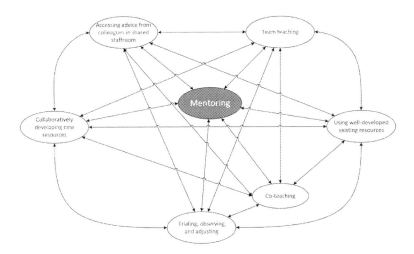

Figure 5.2 Sam: a trellis of PSLs in the Design Department

Table 5.1 provides some examples to help illustrate the type of inter-relationships between PSLs that form a trellis.

Table 5.1 Sam: examples where PSLs inter-relate

	Accessing advice*	Team teaching	Well-prepared resources**	Co-teaching***	Trialling and adjusting
Mentoring	Sam's mentor sometimes facilitates advice from other colleagues	Sam team teaches with his mentor	Provided by the mentor	Sometimes arranged by the mentor	Sam discusses and reflects on approaches and outcomes with his mentor
Accessing advice		Team teaching provides good access to observation and advice	Use and further development of resources discussed	Advice and support shared between co-teachers	Sam discusses and reflects on approaches and outcomes with colleagues

Continued

Trellis of practices that support learning

Table 5.1 (Cont.)

	Accessing advice*	Team teaching	Well-prepared resources**	Co-teaching***	Trialling and adjusting
Team teaching			Well-prepared resources are shared when team teaching	Occasional team teaching with co-teacher	When trialling approaches during team teaching, feedback can occur quickly
Well-prepared resources				Resources are often shared between co-teachers	Approaches and resources are trialled and altered as needed
Co-teaching					Discussion between co-teachers can support trialling and reflecting on new approaches

* Accessing advice and support from colleagues in a shared office space
** Using well-prepared resources
*** Co-teaching is where two teachers teach the same subject in the same semester to a different group of students

A "work site" is not always just a physical site. This has become increasingly the case as a result of the 2020s COVID-19 pandemic. Similarly, PSLs are not necessarily entirely in the physical face-to-face realm. Next, we explore Tamsin's experience, which included some online PSLs.

Vignette 5.4 Tamsin: online PSLs

As you may recall from Chapters 2 and 3, Tamsin is an experienced teacher who has moved into a new teaching area and a new campus about a year ago. She is relatively isolated on her campus. There are no other teachers from the same teaching area on her campus (Regional Campus), and her workstation has been placed in the middle of an open-plan area that houses administrative staff, so easy access to other teachers on her campus is also restricted.

Tamsin has developed several effective practices to support her learning, including undertaking a bachelor's degree in adult education (not a requirement in Australia and usually undertaken by experienced teachers), interacting with the Aboriginal support unit on her campus, and chatting with people from the Information Technology area on another campus (see Chapter 7 for more information about these last two practices). She also undertakes practices that support the learning of other teachers, that she finds also support her own learning, such as volunteering to team teach with other teachers on another campus, mentoring other teachers on another campus, and inviting new teachers to undertake a lesson with her class and providing feedback to them. However, most of these PSLs do not interact with each other. Here we focus on some PSLs that do interact, most of which are accessed online.

Tamsin attends online meetings of her teaching team. These meetings, attended by about 20 teachers each time, take place for about one hour once a fortnight. This regular scheduling allows teachers to know when the next meeting will take place so they can prepare if there is something they want to follow up on. The meetings are facilitated by a Senior Teacher, and the Head of School attends for part of each meeting to "do the management" (Tamsin's words), which usually involves compliance-related information including things such as updates on relevant policies and procedures. After this more formal part of the meeting, the Head of School leaves and the teachers use the remaining time to discuss their teaching. Sometimes one of the teachers presents information about a teaching or assessment approach they are using, and sometimes it is more ad hoc. Tamsin finds this part of the meeting to be valuable. It provides ideas for teaching approaches she can trial, a chance for her to ask questions about any challenges she has, and the opportunity to hear what successes or issues others have had. Sometimes teachers will discuss teaching resources they have developed and share these with others via email. As Tamsin notes, "I rely on the colleagues within my [teaching] programme at the minute to support my learning because that's what I'm trying to learn."

If one of the teachers has presented a teaching or assessment approach that Tamsin is interested in, she contacts them after the meeting via email to arrange a chat. This often results in the sharing of relevant resources. Tamsin gets in touch with colleagues after meetings regularly and quite deliberately to develop relationships with other teachers who she sees as having good teaching approaches. This is also the approach that Tamsin used when she invited one of her colleagues to be her mentor. This mentoring relationship is ongoing and proving valuable in supporting Tamsin's learning. Tamsin trials different approaches, observes the outcome, and makes appropriate adjustments.

Before the COVID-19 pandemic, these teachers could meet face-to-face once a year. In the only annual face-to-face meeting that she has been able to attend, Tamsin took her resources to share with others so that she could get feedback from others and she found this valuable.

So what?

As an experienced teacher, Tamsin has developed a good range of (mostly non-interacting) PSLs across two campuses – her previous campus and her present campus. She has also been very proactive in creating her own trellis of PSLs around the online meeting. Physical isolation has to some extent been overcome by the many and varied PSLs that Tamsin has engaged with. In relation to the trellis of PSLs, while Figure 5.3 shows several inter-related PSLs associated with the online meeting, these cannot be considered to create a strong trellis because each of them is relatively limited in time, interconnectedness, and intensity.

Trellis of practices that support learning

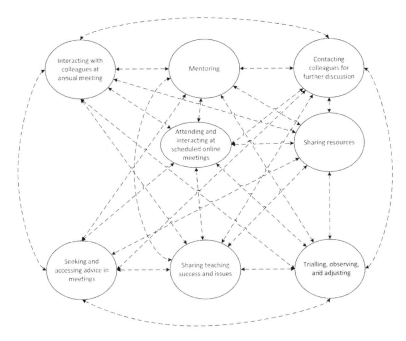

Figure 5.3 Tamsin: an online trellis of PSLs

It is important to note that while Figure 5.3 shows a relatively large number of inter-related PSLs, it is a fragile and flimsy trellis (I have tried to illustrate this through the dotted lines in the trellis). The reasons the trellis is not strong include the limited timespan of each of the PSLs, and the fact that many of the PSLs are not established (either structurally or informally) as ongoing – Tamsin has to actively seek a number of the interactions each time. Compare this with some of the more structured and established PSLs that Sam engages with largely through just turning up to work. Also, for Tamsin, these inter-related PSLs form only a small part of all the PSLs that she engages with. In considering this trellis of PSLs, it is important to remember that Tamsin is an experienced and accomplished teacher. She has been able to benefit from the trellis of PSLs that she has largely developed herself through taking advantage of possibilities. However, this trellis is flimsy and can easily disappear. For a single teacher (even one as accomplished and motivated as Tamsin), developing a trellis of PSLs can be difficult. Chapter 8 provides further discussion related to setting up a trellis of PSLs (hint, collaboration can be powerful).

Next, we consider a stronger trellis of PSLs that includes two mentors.

Trellis of practices that support learning

Vignette 5.5 Alice: a trellis of PSLs with two mentors

The trellis of PSLs that supports Alice's learning is relatively unique in that it has two dedicated mentors at its centre, and each mentor works with Alice in different ways and in relation to different teaching areas. Both mentors are experienced teachers who have been working in the same teaching department for more than a decade, they have a high level of respect for each other, and each knows that the other is also mentoring Alice. Each mentor provides Alice with well-prepared existing teaching and assessment resources, and each has done some team teaching with Alice. Alice interacts with colleagues at the communal table in the staffroom (discussed further in Chapter 7), sharing stories, and asking questions. She also trials new approaches, observes, and makes adjustments based on outcomes (see Figure 5.4).

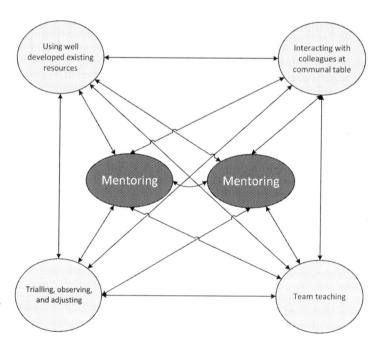

Figure 5.4 Alice: a trellis of PSLs with two mentors

Trellis of practices that support learning

I am not arguing that two mentors are better than one. However, there are circumstances where having two mentors can be beneficial. One benefit for Alice is that she feels she is not taking up too much time for each of her mentors. This can be especially valuable during times of peak workload. She also values being able to get subject specific advice from each of her mentors.

The final vignette outlines the strong trellis of PSLs that is available for Ewan and his colleagues.

Vignette 5.6 Ewan: a strong trellis of PSLs

As Figure 5.5 illustrates, the trellis of PSLs in the Air Conditioning and Refrigeration Department is a sturdy one. Two of the important components of this strong trellis of PSLs are an experienced and dedicated mentor (see Chapter 6), as well as a daily scheduled morning tea (see Chapter 7). When he was a new teacher, Ewan's mentor, David, would team teach with him the first time that he taught a new subject, and initially provided him with well-prepared resources to use. David also facilitates interactions with co-teachers so that they can support each other and reflect together. The staffroom is set up in such a way that interactions between colleagues are ongoing (see Chapter 7). There is also a tradition in the department that resources, assessment items, and teaching approaches are developed collaboratively. Ewan also trials different approaches, observes, and makes adjustments as appropriate.

The Air Conditioning and Refrigeration Department where Ewan works has developed a sturdy and robust trellis of PSLs. This is the work of many years, and is supported by low staff turnover, teachers and managers with higher-level teaching qualifications, and a strong sense of solidarity between colleagues.

Trellis of practices that support learning

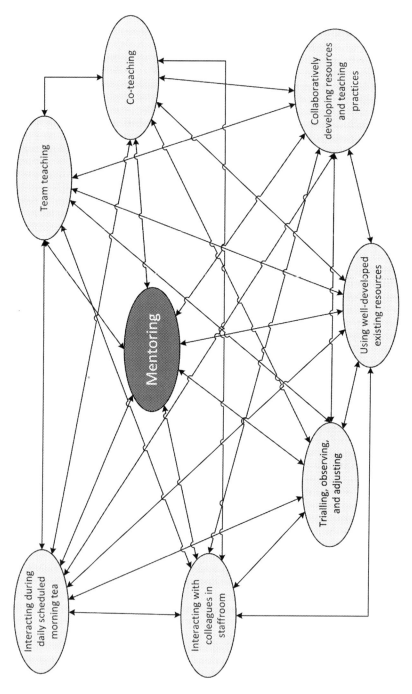

Figure 5.5 Ewan: a strong trellis of PSLs

Concluding comments

While the number of inter-related PSLs is important in developing a strong trellis of PSLs, the quantity of PSLs is not in itself an indication of a strong trellis. As the example involving Tamsin illustrates, two other factors are also important: time and ease of access. It is worth considering the difference between the trellis of PSLs available for Ewan and that available for Tamsin. For Ewan, almost all the PSLs that he engaged with were inter-related. They were also extensive, available daily, and easily accessed. For Tamsin, only a small proportion of the PSLs she engaged with were inter-related, most of the inter-related PSLs were available only for short periods (for example, the fortnightly online meeting, brief phone calls initiated by Tamsin), and most of them required ongoing work on Tamsin's part to access.

Many of the strong trellises of PSLs I have seen were for permanently employed teachers. Special consideration needs to be given to developing a trellis of PSLs for casually employed teachers. A mentor who has an awareness of the practice architectures that enable and constrain casual teacher learning (see Chapter 4) is likely to be in a stronger position to support teacher learning. A trellis of PSLs for casual teachers needs to consider the time costs of some of the PSLs that might be of value (Francisco, 2008). For instance, involvement in the collaborative development of new resources can provide a good learning opportunity for teachers. However, paid time to do this work is rarely provided for casually employed teachers. The focus needs to be on PSLs where the time costs for the casual teacher do not outweigh the benefits. These might include co-teaching, team teaching, mentoring, and accessing well-prepared resources. In my research, all those teachers who had access to a regularly scheduled shared morning tea (regardless of employment basis) found them beneficial to their learning. They also largely enjoyed the times that they were able to attend these, and some mentioned the development of a sense of belonging as a result. So, while scheduled morning teas may be costly in terms of time, for casual teachers, attendance is often considered to be worth the cost.

You will notice that mentoring is a component of each of the trellises of PSLs illustrated in this chapter, and, for all but Tamsin, the mentor serves as a linchpin within the trellis (for Tamsin, the scheduled meeting seems to be the key link). It might be that a trellis of PSLs is possible without a mentor, but I have not seen one. Similarly, in his research with FE teachers in Scotland and Wales, Husband (2020) found that, "respondents repeatedly identified the work of formal and informal mentors as critical to their development" (p. 54). He further found that, "Mentors emerged from the data as the links in the system and the focus of much of the success of the programmes of training" (p. 62). This concept of the mentor as a crucial link between various PSLs is an important one. The next chapter focusses on mentoring.

Questions to consider

For the individual

- What elements of a trellis of practices that support learning (PSLs) do you have in your workplace (this might include a virtual workplace)?
- What approaches that you have read about in this chapter can you introduce in your workplace to enhance the trellis of PSLs?
  - Whose support might you need to gain to be able to do this?

For the organisation

- What elements of a trellis of PSLs are in place in each of the local sites in your organisation?
- What arrangements could be put in place to better support the development of a trellis of PSLs in each site?
  - Who are the people in each site who can support this?

Further reading

Francisco, S. (2020a). Developing a trellis of practices that support learning in the workplace. *Studies in Continuing Education, 42*(1), 102–117.

This article uses the theory of practice architectures to analyse the practices that support VET teacher learning in the workplace.

Francisco, S. (2020b). What novice vocational education and training teachers learn in the teaching workplace. *International Journal of Training Research, 18*(1), 37–54. doi: 10.1080/14480220.2020.1747785

The title says it all really.

Francisco, S. (2017). Mentoring as part of a trellis of practices that support learning. In K. Mahon, S. Francisco, & S. Kemmis (Eds.), *Exploring education and professional practice: through the lens of practice architectures*. Singapore: Springer.

This chapter addresses some of the same issues as this present chapter, but with a stronger focus on mentoring.

References

Francisco, S. (2020). Developing a trellis of practices that support learning in the workplace. *Studies in Continuing Education, 42*(1), 102–117.

Francisco, S. (2017). Mentoring as part of a trellis of practices that support learning. In K. Mahon, S. Francisco, & S. Kemmis (Eds.), *Exploring education and professional practice: through the lens of practice architectures*. Singapore: Springer. doi: 10.1007/978-981-10-2219-7

Francisco, S. (2008). *Professional development: what casual TAFE teachers want*. Australian Vocational Education and Training Research Association conference, April 2008, Adelaide. Refereed conference paper https://avetra.org.au/data/Conference_2008_pres./56._Susanne_Francisco.pdf

Husband, G. (2020). The role of mentors in supporting the professional learning of lecturers in further education colleges in Scotland and Wales. *Research in Post-Compulsory Education, 25*(1), 42–67, doi: 10.1080/13596748.2020.1720167

Husband, G. (2018). The professional learning of further education lecturers: effects of initial lecturer education programmes on continuing professional learning in Scotland and Wales. *Research in Post-Compulsory Education, 23*(2), 159–180, doi: 10.1080/13596748.2018.1444384

Kemmis, S., Edwards-Groves, C., Wilkinson, J., & Hardy, I. (2012). Ecologies of practices. In P. Hager, A. Lee, & A. Reich (Eds.), *Practice, learning and change: practice theory perspectives on professional learning*. Dordrecht: Springer.

Kemmis, S., Wilkinson, J., Edwards-Groves, C., Grootenboer, P., Hardy, I., & Bristol, L. (2014). *Changing practices, changing education*. New York: Springer.

Mahon, K., Kemmis, S., Francisco, S., & Lloyd, A. (2017). Introduction: practice theory and the theory of practice architectures. In K. Mahon, S. Francisco, & S. Kemmis (Eds.), *Exploring education and professional practice: through the lens of practice architectures*. Singapore: Springer.

6 Mentoring

Can you remember a mentor who made a difference to your life? To your understanding? To your actions? To your perceptions of self and others? Mentoring can be a valuable support for professional learning. Mentoring is also an important component of a trellis of practices that support learning (PSLs). This chapter provides an introduction to mentoring. We begin by exploring what mentoring is, and some of the different approaches that can be taken to mentoring. The chapter identifies key characteristics of successful mentoring and outlines the phases of a successful mentoring relationship. Next, we provide an overview of mentoring skills and characteristics, and conclude with some questions to consider concerning mentoring for individuals and organisations.

As you will have seen in previous chapters, mentoring forms a solid basis for the development of teacher learning. In my research, every case where a strong trellis of PSLs was developed involved a strong mentoring relationship. That does not mean that a mentoring relationship automatically results in the development of a solid trellis of PSLs: there were a number of cases in my research where the teacher was part of a valuable mentoring relationship, but this was not inter-related with other PSLs and no trellis of PSLs was developed (Francisco, 2020, 2017).

Mentoring is an approach to professional learning that is flexible. It can be developed to support learning in almost every context and can be designed to meet a range of mentee and organisational needs. In research undertaken into the mentoring of Further Education (FE) teachers in Britain, Hobson et al. (2015) found the following benefits for mentees: "enabling [mentees] to talk about a range of difficulties that they experience; supporting their emotional wellbeing; helping them develop general pedagogical techniques;

and helping develop their subject pedagogy" (p. 47), as well as supporting the development of critical reflection, assisting with access to teaching resources and equipment (p. 49), and support with the development of subject and vocational knowledge (p. 49).

Understandings and practices of mentoring encompass a range of possibilities. This includes approaches such as one-to-one mentoring (see for instance, Zachary, 2012), e-mentoring (see for instance, Owen, 2015), and peer group mentoring (PGM, see for instance, Heikkinen et al., 2012; Kemmis & Heikkinen, 2012; Langelotz, 2017). Here we focus on mentoring that is likely to be of most value within a trellis of PSLs. This involves mentoring that is based on an understanding of adult learning principles (Knowles et al., 2015), and that focusses on the learning goals of the mentee.

We begin by considering induction and developmental mentoring. Induction mentoring occurs when you begin a new job (Pennanen et al., 2016). It is usually associated with being new to an organisation but can also be used when you take on a new role within the organisation that you already work for. Developmental mentoring is usually focussed on supporting teacher development in a particular direction. For instance, if a mentee is seeking to develop their approach to leading, or online teaching, they might seek a mentor to help them focus on their learning goals in that particular area.

Induction mentoring

Induction mentoring can be very important in supporting people to settle into their role. It can affect how teachers feel about their workplace, the skills and knowledge they develop, and whether they choose to stay. In research about the learning of FE teachers in Scotland and Wales, Husband (2018) found that induction mentoring was a valuable component of initial teacher learning.

> An unexpected finding of this study is closely related to the work of mentors in the studied colleges, the influence of informal or perhaps more appropriately, unofficial mentors. The support afforded by colleagues to new members of teams was a consistent theme in the interviews conducted. Where gaps in support and training provision for new lecturers were evident, they were filled (in many

different ways) by colleagues. This finding echoes that reported by Slade (2013) recalling the importance of colleagues in the induction, mentoring and training of public sector workers such as the police. Much of the learning carried out is in practice, embedded into teams and witnessing, participating and enacting the role with a gradual extension of skills and confidence leading towards competence and autonomy.

(pp. 176–177)

Induction mentoring is often associated with a broader induction programme, of which mentoring is just one component. Depending on what the broader induction programme involves, induction mentoring can be of more or less importance in relation to teacher learning and support. Often in Vocational and FE colleges, the induction programme (outside induction mentoring) is limited, and so induction mentoring becomes crucial for supporting teacher learning in their initial weeks and months of being a teacher. Vignette 6.1 below outlines Alice's initial experience of induction mentoring when she began as a teacher in a new college.

Vignette 6.1 Induction mentoring – Alice

In Alice's workplace, the organisation has an induction programme. However, it is limited to paperwork and compulsory compliance training for matters such as work health and safety.

On Alice's first day as a teacher, her supervisor introduced her to Alma, an experienced teacher in the same teaching department. Alma was asked to "show Alice the ropes". Her supervisor had called her into the office to meet Alice as Alma was walking to the coffee shop for her morning coffee, and she invited Alice to join her. They chatted briefly while lining up to order coffee, and then Alice suggested that they sit and drink their coffee so that they could discuss what she was expected to do. Alma could not do this because she was not yet prepared for her next class, starting in less than an hour, and was somewhat curt in letting Alice know that she did not have the time to chat with her. She offered to put together some resources that might be useful for Alice and leave them on her desk. Alice returned to her desk feeling a bit let down, unimpressed with Alma's attitude, and unsure what she needed to do to prepare for teaching the next day. The relationship between Alice and Alma was a strained one over the first few weeks, with Alice asking questions only when she could see no other alternative.

Alma

Before being called into her supervisor's office, Alma had not been advised that she would be expected to provide induction mentoring for Alice. She had some new classes that she had been required to take on because of the illness of another teacher and these were in a teaching area where she had limited knowledge. As a result, Alma had been up late the night before trying to ensure that she understood the content that she was due to teach. Additionally, she was concerned that one of her students was experiencing difficulties with their studies due to a difficult home situation and she was hoping to connect with that student after class. Alma felt overwhelmed just getting through the day and being lumped unexpectedly with a new teacher was the last thing she needed.

So what?

Alma had been given no warning of the expectation that she would mentor Alice. Therefore, she had been unable to prepare for the first meeting or to consider how best to support Alice. She had an excessive workload and was also overloaded emotionally and mentally.

As many of you will know, the scenario where an experienced teacher is asked to mentor a new teacher with no warning, and without considering the capacity of the experienced teacher to do so, is not an isolated one. A quick chat between Alma and the supervisor at least a day or so before meeting Alice may have resulted in a better understanding of Alma's capacity to support Alice that week, and perhaps the supervisor could have found a different induction mentor. Even if the supervisor had insisted that Alma do the mentoring, she would have had time to consider how she might approach the first meeting.

Mentoring

Induction mentoring that has been pre-planned and well organised can form the basis of a well-developed trellis of PSLs. Vignette 6.2 below of Sam's induction mentoring experience is an example of such an arrangement.

Vignette 6.2 Induction mentoring – Sam

Sam's supervisor had arranged for Anne, the coordinator of the area that Sam teaches in, to be his mentor. Anne is an experienced mentor and had prepared for their first meeting. Some years previously, Anne had arranged for the staffroom to be set up so that new teachers are initially placed at a workstation beside her workstation. This allows for ease of access in those crucial first weeks and months. On Sam's first day, his supervisor introduced him to Anne, and Anne showed him to the workstation beside her own. Before his arrival, the supervisor had arranged a range of basic information, including details related to Sam's computer and network access. On the day Sam began work, he was given a short document that provided all the information he needed to set up his computer and access the relevant networks and so on. He was also given a contact number for the IT helpdesk. Anne left Sam at his workstation to settle in and get his network access and set up established, inviting him to join her later that morning for coffee. At the coffee break, Anne suggested that they arrange to meet for coffee most mornings and asked that, where possible, Sam keep a note of questions he had for her and they would discuss these questions over coffee each day.

So what?

Sam's supervisor had prepared for his arrival by discussing it with Anne and checking on her availability to be a mentor. The supervisor had also ensured that relevant administrative arrangements, including those related to computer access, were in place. The supervisor's arrangement with Anne to support new teachers was a longstanding one, and Anne was given formal recognition and teaching release for this (and other) additional work.

Anne was prepared for her induction mentoring role. Nonetheless, she made herself more available to her mentee than is often the case.

> Such availability needs to be managed to ensure that the mentor's workload is not overly impacted. Anne identified some boundaries that she required to enable her to manage her workload, such as asking Sam to keep questions until the morning tea discussion each day.

Induction mentoring can serve a range of purposes, including:

- Support with understanding organisational and local expectations;
- Information about where resources are located and how to access them;
- Support with teaching-related development.

One of the sometimes-overlooked issues that can arise for new teachers is that occasionally they are not made aware of support arrangements available to them. This can be for various reasons, such as a lack of effective communication strategies, or information about such arrangements being provided in the middle of a stack of paperwork that new teachers receive on commencement. Not knowing that specific support arrangements for new teachers exist, or not knowing how to access them, effectively makes such arrangements unavailable. A mentor can be a valuable conduit to help new teachers become aware of opportunities they can access.

Developmental mentoring

Developmental mentoring can be used for a broad range of purposes. Some authors (see for instance, Clutterbuck, 2007) argue that there are two different approaches to developmental mentoring: one where the focus is on the whole career development of the mentee, to sponsor the mentee into a successful career (sometimes referred to as the American model); and the other where the focus is on supporting the mentee to meet (usually self-identified) specific learning goals (sometimes referred to as the European model). Here we focus on the latter. Developmental mentoring can often include activities such as:

- regular mentoring meetings;
- brokering introductions to others who can support the mentee's learning goals;
- identifying work projects that can support mentee learning.

Like induction mentoring, arrangements for developmental mentoring must be discussed and negotiated between the people involved. Vignette 6.3 below outlines Alice's experience of developmental mentoring where the mentor and mentee had quite different expectations and these expectations were not clarified.

Vignette 6.3 Developmental mentoring – Alice

In her second year of teaching, Alice was asked to undertake a large project to develop an online learning programme for a particular qualification. Her skills in this area were limited, but Alice had been so successful in other new areas of work that her supervisor was confident she would also be successful with this new endeavour. The supervisor arranged for Alice to be mentored by Pam, the leader of the online learning team for the organisation. The supervisor and Pam also organised for Alice to have a workstation in the online learning area three days a week. Pam's workload was heavy and she had limited availability to support Alice. Alice had limited additional support to develop her skills and understanding of online learning and did not really know where to begin. Pam was overwhelmed by Alice's needs and, shortly into their relationship, Pam limited her contact with Alice to a brief meeting once a week.

So what?

Alice and Pam went into the mentoring relationship with different expectations about what the mentoring would involve and what each person would do. Alice had high support needs for her learning, and expectations that Pam was the person to meet all those needs. Pam had a demanding job and limited availability to support Alice. She expected that Alice would undertake training courses and use documentation developed by the online learning team to support her learning. Importantly, there were no initial discussions where expectations of the mentoring relationship were negotiated. Both Pam and Alice became unhappy about the mentoring relationship relatively quickly and it disintegrated thereafter.

Mentoring

While Alice and Pam's experiences of a mentoring relationship where each person had very different expectations is not an isolated one, most of the mentoring relationships that were apparent in my research were positive experiences for both the mentor and mentee. The vignette below of Ewan's experiences provides an example of a successful mentoring relationship that was set up well right from the beginning.

Vignette 6.4 Developmental mentoring – Ewan

Ewan has a seasoned mentor, who had been mentoring both new and experienced teachers for many years. In addition to his extensive experience, David had undertaken the mentor training programme when it was offered about two years before Ewan started work as a teacher in his area. David is therefore familiar with the notion of phases of a mentoring relationship and has supported Ewan through the preparation and negotiation phases before settling into a mentoring phase. David arranged for a range of support strategies such as bringing Ewan in on resource development work from the beginning of his employment, and team teaching with him on some subjects. After only two months of induction mentoring (a relatively short period for induction mentoring), Ewan and David agreed to transition to a developmental mentoring arrangement focussed on particular learning goals.

So what?

The teaching department that Ewan was teaching in had a long tradition of valuing and supporting mentoring. This tradition of overt valuing of mentoring (and other arrangements that supported ongoing teacher development) was powerful within this teaching team and resulted in strong and relatively rapid teacher development.

Formal or informal mentoring

Whether a mentoring relationship is considered "formal" or "informal" is not necessarily an indicator of success. When a mentoring relationship is described as formal it usually means that it has been established as part of an organisational or local mentoring programme. Where it is described as informal it usually means that it is an arrangement that has been developed between the mentor and mentee. Ewan and David (Vignette 6.4) considered themselves to be in an informal mentoring relationship because it was outside the broader organisational mentoring programme. However, David was an experienced mentor and had continued to develop his skills and knowledge in mentoring through training and discussions with his own mentor. Relevant literature related to formal and informal mentoring (Boud & Rooney, 2018; Colley et al., 2003) raises a number of issues that are better addressed on their own than through the lens of whether the mentoring is considered to be "formal" or "informal". One of these issues is whether the mentoring is expected to focus on the needs of the organisation or individual. Like so many dualistic arguments, where one focus is set up as the opposite of the other, the most effective outcome likely rests in some combination of the two. In a mentoring arrangement that focusses on the learning goals of the mentee, these goals are usually informed both by the requirements of the organisation and the development needs and wishes of the individual. The key point is that the requirements of the organisation do not come directly from the mentor. They come from a range of places, such as expectations of the organisation concerning promotion, key performance indicators (where the organisation has these), performance management meetings, organisational documentation related to position descriptions and expected capabilities, and more general influences related to the culture of the organisation. Together with personal development aspirations and expectations, these organisational expectations influence the development of a mentee's learning goals.

Another issue often hidden within the "formal/informal" dualism is whether the mentor has received any training or related skill development. As seen in Ewan's Vignette 6.4, being in an informal mentoring relationship does not necessarily mean that the mentor has not been involved in mentor development or training. Often a formal mentoring programme also increases the number of informal mentoring relationships undertaken in the organisation.

Developing the structures for successful mentoring

Whether mentoring is considered formal (as part of an acknowledged programme), or informal (where an agreement is made between the mentor

Mentoring

and mentee), there are several factors that increase the chances of success. In research into mentoring of FE teachers in Britain, Cunningham (2007) and Hobson et al. (2015) identify the importance of organisational factors in supporting successful mentoring, highlighting the following key factors:

- an overt commitment to mentoring by the organisation
- a culture of collegiality within the organisation
- the provision of resources to support mentoring
- the provision of dedicated time for mentoring
- a commitment to ongoing development for mentors.

Similarly, Zachary and Koestenbaum (2005) highlight the importance of developing a mentoring culture within an organisation.

While an organisational culture that values and supports mentoring increases the chances of success, it is important to note that a successful mentoring relationship is possible without organisational support, and strong organisational support for mentoring does not guarantee that an individual mentoring relationship will be successful.

Mentoring and adult learning principles

Adult learning principles are an important component of a successful mentoring relationship. Knowles et al. (2015) identified six key adult learning principles:

- adults need to know why they are learning something
- adults are self-directed in their learning (more about this shortly)
- the prior experience of the learner is important
- adults are more likely to learn when they have a need to do so and are ready to learn
- orientation to learning
- adults usually learn best when they have an internal motivation to learn.

These principles are valuable in informing the development of mentoring arrangements at an individual mentoring relationship level as well as at a mentoring programme level. A well-designed mentoring relationship can readily address the adult learning principles (see also *Phases of a Mentoring Relationship* later in this chapter). Below is a brief discussion of each of the adult learning principles and relevant mentoring approaches. Further information about the adult learning principles can be found in Knowles et al. (2015).

Adults need to know why they are learning something

If the mentoring relationship is developed based on the learning goals of the mentee this principle is usually addressed.

Adults are self-directed in their learning

This is the adult learning principle that has had the most criticism (see for instance, Brookfield, 1984). Some adults are not self-directing in their learning and might need some support to develop the skills required to be self-directing. It is also possible that some mentees will prefer to take a dependant role initially and will need to be supported to become more independent in their learning.

The prior experience of the learner is important

A recognition of mentee experiences, skills, and abilities is an important component of a mentoring relationship. Where mentee experiences have not been positive, a mentor might be able to support critical reflection on those experiences and help with future positive development.

Adults learn when they are ready and when they have a need to do so

Ensuring that a mentoring relationship is voluntary goes some way toward addressing this principle. Mentoring is inherently likely to meet this adult learning principle when the mentoring relationship is designed based on the learning goals of the mentee and when the focus is on the needs of the mentee.

Orientation to learning

This principle is likely to be met where there is a clear relationship between what is being learnt and the work that the mentee is involved with or wants to become involved with.

Internal motivation to learn

This principle relates to the mentee's motivation for ongoing professional (and personal) development. Again, mentee development of their own learning goals strongly supports this adult learning principle.

Adult learning principles can be deliberately incorporated into a mentoring programme or an individual mentoring relationship by understanding the phases of a mentoring relationship.

Phases of a mentoring relationship

Much of the mentoring literature identifies different phases of a mentoring relationship (see for instance, Ragins & Kram, 2007; Zachary, 2012). Clearly identifying and establishing deliberate phases in a mentoring relationship can be beneficial in supporting successful mentoring. These phases can be identified as preparation, negotiation, mentoring for growth, and closure and redefinition.

A *preparation* phase, which takes place before the first meeting, enables the mentor to determine if they have the time, the willingness, and the capacity to be a mentor at that time and in that context. As was apparent in the Alice vignette 6.1, there was no preparation phase. In developmental mentoring especially, the preparation phase is also a time when a mentee can begin to identify their learning goals, and to consider how the mentor might be able to support them in meeting those goals. Mentee learning goals are usually informed by the needs and expectations of the organisation that they work for, as well as by individual interests and needs for growth and development.

The *negotiation* phase takes place during the first few meetings. During this phase, the mentor and mentee agree about factors such as the regularity and place of meetings, the level of confidentiality of the meetings, and – importantly – what to meet about. During the negotiation phase, the mentor and mentee discuss their understanding of what success will look like. Discussions are held about the mentee's learning goals, with the mentor supporting the mentee to develop achievable and specific learning goals. For instance, a mentee will often come to the first meeting with a broad goal such as "becoming a better teacher". The mentor might then support them to develop more specific and measurable goals such as:

- develop their approach to supporting student group work
- create a number of authentic assessment tasks
- develop a number of specific resources that support student learning;

and so on.

It is in the negotiation phase that the mentor and mentee begin to develop trust in each other. The development of relational trust can be an important component of a successful mentoring relationship.

The *mentoring for growth* phase is the phase that we traditionally understand as mentoring. During this phase, the mentor and mentee focus on the mentee's learning goals. Regular meetings are usually held during this phase. Strategies for ensuring these meetings are focused on the needs and learning goals of the mentee might include:

- opportunities for the mentee to debrief about a particular incident
- the mentor challenging the mentee to push themselves further
- the mentee reporting on changes put in place since the previous meeting and the success or otherwise of those changes
- determining future actions
- the mentor supporting the mentee to engage in reflection on their professional practice.[1]
- Regularly returning to the mentee's learning goals and discussing progress toward meeting those goals.

The following administrative approaches can also be useful.

- The mentee sending an email within 24 hours of each meeting:
  - outlining the key issues addressed in the meeting
  - clearly identifying agreed actions to be undertaken by the mentee and the mentor. This often forms the starting point for the next meeting.

---

1 Reflection is an important aspect of mentoring meetings. Critical reflection is always more than 'having a think about it'. There are a range of approaches that can be taken to support reflection. Stephen Brookfield's book, Becoming a Critically Reflective Teacher (2017), provides a good approach to supporting critical reflection. He identifies four lenses to support critical reflection: student feedback, peer feedback, relevant literature, and autobiographical lens. See Chapter 8 of this book for further discussion of reflection.

- A regular meeting day and time. For instance, every second Tuesday at 2.00 pm. If the meeting needs to be postponed, another meeting time needs to be arranged. In my research I have found that, if a new meeting time is not arranged, mentees are often reluctant to "bother" their (usually busy) mentors with requests for a meeting. Establishing a regular meeting time helps with this issue, as does the expectation that a new appointment is made if a meeting has to be postponed.
- In many contexts, it is advantageous if mentoring meetings can take place outside the work area. This might include meetings in a coffee shop, or even another room that is not usually used as part of the day-to-day work. One reason for this is to prevent being interrupted by phone calls, student or colleague queries, or other day-to-day work. Another reason is that it allows more freedom for broader discussions and even blue sky thinking when removed from the usual physical work environment.

The *closure and redefinition* phase is an important one, however, it is often overlooked. At a basic level the framework for the closure phase can be established during the negotiation phase. This is done by agreeing on an end date for the mentoring relationship. The actual time will vary according to local contexts and individual needs. For induction mentoring this might be three–four months or as little as one month, depending on the needs of the mentee and the availability of the mentor. For developmental mentoring it might be 12 months. In teaching departments, it is often for the duration of the academic year. If, however, the learning goals are met before the agreed end date, closure might occur earlier. Other common reasons for early closure include incompatibility between mentor and mentee, one person getting a job elsewhere, or the mentor having an increased workload or other obligations that result in their decreased ability to be a mentor.

Whatever the reason for early closure (even if it relates to incompatibility of the mentor and mentee), the following things will assist in a positive outcome:

- a discussion of what the mentee has learnt as a result of the mentoring relationship, especially in relation to their learning goals
    - where possible (and depending on the reasons for the end of the relationship) it can be useful to identify the mentee's new learning goals,

and the mentor might even be able to support them in addressing those learning goals
- celebration of the mentee's learning
- gratitude to the mentor for supporting that learning.

After a mentoring arrangement is over, there is necessarily a redefinition of the relationship between the mentor and the mentee. Overtly acknowledging this redefinition can be useful. It might be that the mentor and mentee become personal friends or identify as colleagues.

Further considerations

In this section we consider e-mentoring, establishing specialist mentors, and the issues associated with a supervisor as a mentor.

E-mentoring

With changes experienced as a result of the COVID-19 pandemic, including increased online learning, teachers are now more than ever working in sites that are physically separated from their colleagues. In addition to supporting mentees to meet their learning goals, e-mentoring is an approach that can decrease people's sense of isolation and provide support in circumstances where face-to-face mentoring is not a viable option, or where the most appropriate mentor is not in the same physical site as the mentee.

E-mentoring is not new. However, it is increasingly becoming a viable option for Vocational Education and Training (VET) and FE teachers. It can be particularly valuable for teachers working in regional areas where access to experienced mentors might be limited. Hobson et al. (2015) note that, for FE teachers in Britain, "some staff are isolated from support due to the location of their work, part-time working and/or being the only subject expert in their team" (p. 23). Many of the same issues and approaches apply as for face-to-face mentoring. In my research in Australia, a number of regionally based teachers used e-mentoring to support their learning. In each case, the teacher arranged the mentoring herself rather than it being something organised by the organisation that they worked for. Also, in each case the teacher found it a valuable support for them to learn "how to go on" in their work. Vignette 6.5 outlines the experiences of one of these teachers.

Vignette 6.5 E-mentoring – Tamsin

Tamsin teaches at a small regional campus that is about an hour away from where she lives. She takes a proactive approach to further developing her relationships with colleagues, some of whom she has never met face-to-face. Across the Australian state where Tamsin lives and works there are about 20 other teachers in her teaching area who work in regional settings in the same way as her. Their manager has arranged a fortnightly online meeting where teachers can discuss issues associated with their work. One teacher is asked to present at each meeting about a successful teaching-related approach they have undertaken. Often, after a meeting, Tamsin contacts the person who was the presenter at the meeting and discusses their work further. After one such discussion with a teacher called Fiona, Tamsin realised that she could learn a lot from Fiona about supporting the learning of students with literacy issues. When Tamsin got in touch a week later and invited Fiona to be her mentor, Fiona accepted.

So what?

There are several aspects to consider here. The first aspect is a positive one. The manager established arrangements for regular online meetings of all teachers in the teaching area, and these meetings allow the sharing of different aspects of teachers' professional practice and allow for the teachers to come to know each other. A less positive aspect is that Tamsin had to make the mentoring arrangements herself to get the support she needs because there is no mentoring programme available in her organisation. A third aspect is that the additional work that Fiona undertakes as a mentor is not recognised by the organisation and does not result in decreased work in other areas. The last of these could have been addressed by Fiona receiving teaching release hours for her additional work. This is also likely to have resulted in an increase in experienced teachers being willing to mentor others.

Many mentoring arrangements in Vocational and FE depend on volunteerism. That is, experienced teachers mentoring others in addition to their (often already heavy) workload. Volunteerism is largely successful because teachers generally are people who enjoy supporting the learning of others, including their colleagues. However, volunteerism is most likely to occur when the teachers regularly interact with each other and this is more likely when working in the same physical location. There is sometimes resistance to mentoring in formal mentoring programmes where there is no teaching release hours or other workload arrangements made to acknowledge the mentoring workload. This resistance tends to be greater where teachers are not physically working in the same site. Tamsin was able to overcome this by deliberately developing a relationship with Fiona.

Mentors specialising in particular areas

One practice that is successful in some teaching departments is to ask experienced teachers to nominate an area of expertise that they would like to specialise in, and to become a mentor in that area. For instance, an area of industry expertise such as hair colouring for Hairdressing teachers, or an area of teaching expertise such as the development of authentic assessment tasks. This approach can be undertaken in three stages:

1. The experienced teacher (A) is supported to further develop their expertise in their nominated area (for instance, hair colouring).
2. Teacher A mentors teacher B in hair colouring.
3. Teachers A and B mentor new teachers in hair colouring.

Specialised mentoring arrangements can be valuable; however, there are several issues to be aware of. These include:

- If mentoring is compulsory:
  - Not everyone is good at mentoring. While most people can become a good mentor if they are willing to learn, we need to acknowledge that some people are unwilling to do so.
  - It is better if people can self-select into a mentoring role.
- If mentoring is voluntary:
  - Those who choose to mentor might be effectively penalised through having a heavier workload than those who do not.

- This can be mitigated by identifying a number of tasks that need to be undertaken, with experienced teachers required to undertake one of them. Mentoring would then become one of various options.
- The risk of one person being the "expert" in a particular area over many years impeding the development of new approaches. While this risk is not usually a strong one, it is something to be aware of.

Peer group mentoring (PGM) – Finnish style

Peer group mentoring (PGM) can refer to a number of different approaches. Here I refer to the PGM that was developed, and is now widely used, in Finland (see for instance Heikkinen et al., 2012). Kemmis and Heikkinen (2012) identify PGM as a "hybrid of practices" (p. 144). It includes mentoring as it is more traditionally understood, as well as coaching. It also includes networking with colleagues, reflecting on aspects of professional practice with colleagues, and the Scandinavian practice of "study circles" where groups of 8–12 people work together over a number of weeks or months to address a particular issue that is relevant to them all. PGM usually involves at least one experienced facilitator as well as a number of relatively new teachers. It can provide induction support for new teachers as well as support for more experienced teachers to try new approaches and address difficult issues.

Supervisors as mentors

Supervisors are often expected to, or choose to, take on the role of mentor for one or more of the staff that they work with. Hobson et al. (2015), in research undertaken with British FE teachers, found that almost half of all respondents to their mentoring survey had been mentored by a line manager (p. 41). This dual role of supervisor and mentor can sometimes be a difficult one to balance, with different relationship expectations for each role. In relation to the mentoring of FE trainee teachers by their direct supervisors, Hobson et al. (2015) note that "This creates tensions between the non-judgemental support advocated in most models of mentoring and organisational performance requirements" (p. 18). It is therefore often recommended that – where possible – these roles be separated. Where one person undertakes both roles, one strategy that could be used is to have supervision and mentoring meetings in different physical locations. For instance, supervision in the office, and mentoring in a coffee shop.

Developing the capability to mentor others

Support, challenge, vision, and trust are four important components of successful mentoring (Daloz, 1999; Francisco & Darwin, 2007; Klasen & Clutterbuck, 2002; Zachary, 2012). The development of a successful mentoring relationship that includes these components requires a range of skills, personal attributes, and understandings, and involves using a range of strategies and approaches. There is a danger that experienced and competent teachers (or other workers) are considered to somehow automatically have mentoring skills and knowledge. Mentoring is a complex, multi-faceted practice and not something that people just somehow know how to do well.

So, what makes a good mentor, and how can a mentor develop the required skills and attributes?

Useful skills and characteristics for mentors

Table 6.1 introduces useful skills for mentoring (Francisco & Darwin, 2007; Zachary 2012). As you read through these it is worth considering which of these you feel you have. And which of these you would value in a mentor. Perhaps use a star rating, with *, **, or *** to represent the importance of each for you.

Table 6.1 Mentor skills and characteristics

Broad characteristics	Associated skills	Skills I have	Skills I want to develop	Skills I want my mentor to have
Communication and relationship building	Listening; Building relationships; Maintaining relationships; Managing conflict; Communicating; Feedback – giving and receiving; Networking			

Table 6.1 (Cont.)

Broad characteristics	Associated skills	Skills I have	Skills I want to develop	Skills I want my mentor to have
Personal attributes	Enthusiasm; Openness to new ideas; Empathy; Valuing difference; Commitment to own learning; Interest in helping others; Approachable			
Emotional intelligence	Self-awareness; Awareness of others' needs;* Encouraging; Supportive			
Experience and knowledge	Relevant professional experience; Goal setting skills; Ability to broker relationships; Problem solving skills; Coaching skills; Reflective practice and ability to support others to develop reflective practice; Organisational knowledge and understanding 'the way things work around here'			

Adapted and developed from Francisco and Darwin (2007).

* This skill involves an awareness of what is appropriate in any given meeting. For instance, when to provide support, when to provide challenge, and when to just listen.

Note, some of the skills identified in one row are also relevant in another row, especially in the 'Communication and relationship building' and the 'Emotional intelligence' rows.

The skills in Table 6.1 are all skills that can be learnt, fostered, and developed. It is very unlikely that someone will have all (or even most) of these skills when they first become a mentor – like teaching, mentoring is a practice of ongoing development. Table 6.1 includes the column 'Skills I want my mentor to have' to help you reflect on what you want from your mentor, and how this might influence the development of your mentoring capabilities.

Mentoring

Mentors can almost always benefit from training. Even people who are experienced mentors sometimes fall into practices that are not in keeping with adult learning principles. This includes talking extensively about their own experiences and areas of expertise without regard to the specific interests and needs of their mentee. A mentor who aims for the mentee to do most of the talking (80% or so) during their meetings, with some well-placed questions or reflections, is likely to better support their mentee's learning than a mentor who talks at length about something they think might be useful for the mentee to know.

Mentor development (which might include a dedicated training workshop) that focusses on adult learning principles can help mentors to:

- understand the phases of a mentoring relationship;
  - including the practices to be undertaken in each phase.
- establish phases of a mentoring relationship;
- understand skills and characteristics that support successful mentoring;
- evaluate their existing mentoring skills and areas for development;
  - Table 6.1 can provide a starting point for this.

Two valuable ways to develop mentoring skills are to be a mentor and to have a mentor.

In seeking a mentor, consider your learning goals and who might be best able to support you in attaining those goals. In each of the mentoring programmes I have helped establish, some of the most accomplished people in the organisations received few or no requests to be a mentor. When I interviewed mentees, they revealed that they had not considered those people as possible mentors for two main reasons: first, they had expected they would have been inundated with requests; and, second, they didn't think the mentors would be prepared to work with them. It is worth considering this when determining who to approach as a mentor and aim for the person who you consider would be the very best mentor you could have. It might be that they are not available, but it is worth asking.

I teach a graduate certificate subject *Mentoring and Workplace Learning for Vocational Education and Training Teachers*. Each time I teach it I find that even well qualified, competent, and experienced teachers and managers are often reluctant to begin taking on a mentoring role because of a lack of confidence in their capabilities. If this is you, I suggest beginning as an induction mentor. Induction mentoring is relatively short-term and requires a willingness to provide support as well as an understanding of basic local arrangements and systems (such as how to arrange photocopying).

Practice architectures that enable and constrain mentoring

In this chapter we have, so far, not focussed explicitly on practice architectures that enable and constrain mentoring, although with a heightened understanding of the concept you have perhaps identified the different practice architectures that have been in evidence in the vignettes. Like all practices, mentoring practices are enabled and constrained by the practice architectures of the site. The practice architectures can be illustrated using the examples throughout the chapter. Cultural-discursive arrangements related to the valuing of mentoring, the purposes of mentoring, and the language associated with mentoring, enable and constrain particular practices. Material-economic arrangements that enable and constrain particular practices associated with mentoring include whether mentors receive teaching time release for mentoring or whether there is an expectation of volunteerism; whether mentor and mentee are in the same physical space; where mentoring takes place such as in the workplace or in a more social environment such as a coffeeshop; what training and support mentors receive, and all of the arrangements associated with how mentoring is established (remember the contrast between Alice and Alma's experiences outlined in Vignette 6.1 and Sam and Anne's experiences outline in Vignette 6.2). Social-political arrangements that enable and constrain particular practices associated with mentoring include understandings about who can be mentored and for what purposes, and who can – and even who is required to – be a mentor. These examples are not exhaustive. They are included as a reminder that the practice architectures of a site enable and constrain particular mentoring practices, and even whether mentoring takes place at all.

Concluding comments

A mentoring relationship can form an important part of a trellis of practices that support learning (PSLs). A mentor who is aware of the value of a trellis of PSLs can actively work to help build such a trellis in their local site (whether that "site" is physical or virtual). This is explored in more detail in Chapter 8.

Questions to consider

For the individual

- What value might a mentor provide for you personally?
  - What learning goals do you have right now that a mentor could support you with?
- Can you identify potential mentors in your organisation that you see as being able to support your learning goals?
  - What professional and interpersonal skills do they have to be able to support you in a mentoring relationship?

For the organisation

- What value might a mentoring programme in your workplace provide for teachers?
- Would it be possible to establish, or further develop, a mentoring programme in your workplace?
  - What might this involve?
  - What are the barriers and how can these be overcome?
  - Who would you need to sponsor such a development?
- If a mentoring programme is established in your workplace, what arrangements can be made to support teachers who are employed on a casual basis?
  - What about casual teachers who are mentors? Is there an arrangement for them to be compensated for this work?

Further reading

Hobson, A. J., Maxwell, B., Stevens, A., Doyle, K., & Malderez, A. (2015). Mentoring and coaching for teachers in the Further Education and Skills sector in England. www.gatsby.org.uk/uploads/education/reports/pdf/mentoring-full-report.pdf

The name says it all really. This paper reports on research about the mentoring of FE teachers in England. The final chapter provides recommendations for supporting successful mentoring arrangements at a local and national level.

Zachary, L. (2012). *The mentor's guide: facilitating effective learning relationships* (2nd ed.). San Francisco, CA: Jossey-Bass.

This book provides mentors with a solid foundation for setting up and maintaining a successful mentoring relationship. It also includes useful "how to" guides such as tips for providing feedback. It provides resources that are useful for individual mentors and these resources could also be used as part of a training programme for mentors.

References

Boud, D., & Rooney, D. (2018). The potential and paradox of informal learning. In Gerhard Messman, Mien Segers, & Philip Dochy (Eds.), *Informal learning at work: triggers, antecedents and consequences*. London: Routledge.

Brookfield, S. (2017). *Becoming a critically reflective teacher* (2nd ed.). San Francisco, CA: John Wiley.

Brookfield, S. (1984). Self-directed learning: a critical paradigm. *Adult Education Quarterly, 35*, 59–71.

Clutterbuck, D. (2007). An international perspective on mentoring. In B. E. Ragin & K. E. Kram (Eds.), *The handbook of mentoring at work: theory, research and practice*. London: Sage.

Colley, H., Hodkinson, P., & Malcom, J. (2003). *Informality and formality in learning: a report for the Learning and Skills Research Centre*. Report, Learning and Skills Research Centre, London.

Cunningham, B. (2007). All the right features: towards an 'architecture' for mentoring trainee teachers in UK further education colleges. *Journal of Education for Teaching, 33*(1), 83–97.

Daloz, L. (1999). *Mentor: guiding the journey of adult learners*. San Francisco, CA: Jossey-Bass.

Francisco, S. (2020). Developing a trellis of practices that support learning in the workplace. *Studies in Continuing Education, 42*(1), 102–117.

Francisco, S. (2017). Mentoring as part of a trellis of practices that support learning. In K. Mahon, S. Francisco, & S. Kemmis (Eds.), *Exploring education and professional practice – through the lens of practice architectures*. Singapore: Springer.

Francisco, S. & Darwin, S. (2007). Mentoring TAFE teachers: support, challenge, vision and trust. *Australian Vocational Education and Training Research Association conference*, April 2007, Melbourne. Refereed conference paper. www.avetra.org.au/data/Conference_2007_pres./46._Susanne_Francisco.pdf

Heikkinen, H. L. T., Jokinen, H., & Tynjälä, P. (2012). *Peer-group mentoring for teacher development*. London: Routledge.

Hobson, A. J., Maxwell, B., Stevens, A., Doyle, K., & Malderez, A. (2015). *Mentoring and coaching for teachers in the Further Education and Skills sector in*

England: full report. London: Gatsby Charitable Foundation, www.gatsby.org. uk/uploads/education/reports/pdf/mentoring-full-report.pdf

Husband, G. (2018). The professional learning of further education lecturers: effects of initial lecturer education programmes on continuing professional learning in Scotland and Wales. *Research in Post-Compulsory Education, 23*(2), 159–180. doi: 10.1080/13596748.2018.1444384

Kemmis, S. & Heikkinen, H. L. T. (2012). Future perspectives: peer group mentoring and international practices for teacher development. In H. L. T. Heikkinen, H. Jokinen, & P. Tynjälä (Eds.), *Peer-group mentoring for teacher development.* London: Routledge.

Klasen, N. & Clutterbuck, D. (2002). Implementing mentoring schemes: a practical guide to successful programs. Oxford: Butterworth Heinemann.

Knowles, M., Holton, E., & Swanson, R. (2015). The adult learner: the definitive classic in adult education and human development (8th ed.). London: Routledge.

Langelotz, L. (2017). Collegial mentoring for professional development. In K. Mahon, S. Francisco, & S. Kemmis (Eds.), *Exploring education and professional practice – through the lens of practice architectures.* Singapore: Springer.

Owen, H. D. (2015). Making the most of mobility: virtual mentoring and education practitioner professional development. *Research in Learning Technology, 23*, 1–14.

Pennanen, M., Bristol, L., Wilkinson, J., & Heikkinen, H. (2016). What is "good" mentoring? Understanding mentoring practices of teacher induction through case studies of Finland and Australia. *Pedagogy, Culture and Society, 24*(1), 27–53.

Ragins, B. & Kram, K. (2007). The roots and meaning of mentoring. In B. E. Ragin & K. E. Kram (Eds.), *The handbook of mentoring at work: theory, research and practice.* Thousand Oaks, CA: Sage.

Zachary, L. (2012). The mentor's guide: facilitating effective learning relationships (2nd ed.). San Francisco, CA: Jossey-Bass.

Zachary, L. & Koestenbaum, P. (2005). *Creating a mentoring culture: the organization's guide.* San Francisco, CA: John Wiley.

Learning in in-between spaces
Creating communicative learning spaces

In previous chapters, we have discussed teacher learning in the workplace. In this chapter, we focus on a specific aspect of workplace learning – learning in in-between spaces. The chapter outlines and discusses the concept of in-between spaces (Solomon et al., 2006), identifies how in-between spaces can be created, and illustrates how some common workplace arrangements can unintentionally shut down in-between spaces. In this chapter, you are also introduced to the concept of communicative learning spaces (Sjolie et al., 2019), and how in-between spaces can become communicative learning spaces.

In-between spaces

In-between spaces are those spaces (physical and temporal) that are in-between the professional and the personal. These are spaces where teachers can interact with colleagues in a relaxed way. Solomon et al. (2006) found learning in in-between spaces in early work that they did when investigating the workplace learning of Vocational Education and Training (VET) teachers. In their research they identified in-between spaces in workrooms, tearooms, and in one instance a car when an in-between space was created through colleagues carpooling to and from work. In-between spaces are connected with the workplace in some way. They might be physically located in the workplace (such as a staff tearoom), on the way to and from work (such as the carpooling example), or take place "in-between" the workday such as at a coffee shop where colleagues share a break from work.

Solomon et al. (2006) found that the lunchroom was an important in-between space for many of the VET teachers in their research. They note,

DOI: 10.4324/9781003112624-7

Learning in in-between spaces

"The lunchroom can be thought of as in-between on-the-job and off-the-job. And again, there is learning occurring. Indeed, it is learning that can significantly contribute to the productivity and effectiveness of this organisation" (p. 8). In in-between spaces, the discussion flows between the personal ("How is your daughter going with her music lessons?") and the professional ("How did that new approach go in class yesterday?"). Solomon et al. found that for one group of VET teachers they were working with:

> There was general consensus among this group that tearoom chats provided spaces where it was 'safe' to say things that couldn't be said in other situations. This group, and several others, told us that tea room chat went in many directions. There was an intermingling of work and non-work topics. It was a space where problems and ideas were 'brought in', exemplified by one worker telling us about 3am thoughts and how he took them to the tea room the following day: 'Guess what I thought of last night?', he would ask.
>
> (p. 10)

In Solomon et al.'s (2006) research, lunchtime was highlighted as the time when much of the in-between spaces chat took place. In my research some years later, morning tea was the most significant time.

Another place where Solomon et al. (2006) found in-between spaces were sometimes created was related to professional development sessions that teachers attended. The teachers spoke about professional development sessions where they felt they learnt little from the actual sessions, but they valued the discussions and learning that took place with colleagues during the breaks (p. 10). Similarly, in research that I did with novice teachers, some teachers noted that the value of the compulsory training courses they attended lay in the discussions with colleagues over morning tea and lunch rather than the courses themselves.

In my research with VET teachers, I found various sites where in-between spaces were regularly created and where teachers learnt quickly and well (examples are provided later in this chapter). However, I also found some teaching departments where in-between spaces were not available. This was especially the case for casually employed teachers. Vignette 7.1 reveals an environment where there were no in-between spaces to support the learning of Sarah, a casually employed teacher.

Vignette 7.1 Elimination of in-between spaces – Sarah

Sarah was employed on a sessional basis (casual employment) to teach Business Administration. In her first year of teaching, she team taught with Wanda, an experienced teacher who also undertook the role of Sarah's mentor. Sarah was teaching 9–14 hours a week, and this was her only employment. All permanently employed teachers in the Business Administration teaching team were based on the second floor of a building that housed their offices and staffroom. Sarah and all casually employed teachers were permitted to use the "casual teachers' office", which included two desks and was dominated by cabinets that held hard copies of outdated teaching resources that were no longer used. Casual teachers rarely spent any time in this office because it was cramped and otherwise not a pleasant environment. Importantly, the casual teachers' office was in another building about ten minutes' walk from the permanent teachers' offices. To further complicate things, Sarah had not been introduced to the permanent teachers from her department. Sarah was heavily reliant on Wanda's support as she was learning to become a teacher. When I visited her in the casual teachers' office it became apparent that she was completely isolated from all other teachers and had no access to teaching-related discussions (either as a participant or as an observer/bystander) or any other ad hoc interactions with teachers other than Wanda. Sarah also rarely interacted with other casual teachers, partly because the casual teachers' office was so unattractive and no-one chose to use it. There were also no established arrangements where casual teachers could meet each other and so they could pass each other in a corridor and not know they were both teachers.

So what?

While the arrangements that Sarah encountered were not intentionally set up to disadvantage casually employed teachers, it would be difficult to deliberately develop arrangements that were more successful in removing the chances of Sarah having access to an in-between space that might support her learning.

Sarah's is an extreme case, however, in my research I found that most casually employed teachers did not have workstations in the same areas as the permanently employed teachers. This was especially the case in the teaching departments that had a high teacher turnover. By separating casual and permanent teachers, the chances for casual teachers to learn through overhearing teaching discussions, or to observe experienced teachers preparing for teaching, or to have a chance to ask ad hoc questions are reduced. This raises the question of whether the high teacher turnover was partly due to the casually employed teachers being separated from the permanently employed teachers and therefore not readily having access to support from their colleagues, or whether permanent teachers in areas of high staff turnover protected themselves by ensuring casual teachers were housed separately to them. The answer is likely to include elements of both.

In Vignette 7.2 below, we see an in-between space created around a large communal table. In many of the vignettes in this chapter, a large communal table forms a physical place where an in-between space is developed. It is worth noting that in my research there were also a (limited) number of teaching areas where there were large communal tables that were rarely used and that did not support the development of an in-between space. As you will have seen in Chapter 4, it is not just the physical arrangements that enable the development or the maintenance of practices.

Vignette 7.2 Communal table – Alice

The staffroom in the Community Services Department where Alice was a teacher was largely open-plan with teachers' workstations divided from each other by a partial partition. At one end of the staffroom, and separated from the teachers' workstations, was a large table. Teachers walked past this table each time they entered or left the staffroom. They also ate their lunch there, had a coffee there, and for some of the teachers it was a place where they prepared lessons, developed resources, and marked assignments. Alice reported that she often sat at the table with other teachers to debrief after a lesson, share successes, hear about the experiences of other teachers, and seek advice. Alice noted:

> I was involved regularly in discussions about development of materials, and with other colleagues there. So I did feel very included and I did feel that what I had to offer was taken on board.

One teacher in particular (James) could usually be found at this table and always welcomed a chat. James was one of Alice's mentors and having easy access to him regularly was valuable in supporting Alice's learning.

The Community Services Department had a tradition of sharing resources, developing resources together, and deep discussions about teaching and assessment approaches. Much of this took place at the communal table.

So what?

This ad hoc arrangement, facilitated by the communal table that all teachers walked past on entry and exit from the staffroom, together with the regular presence of the experienced teacher, James, not only supported Alice's learning but also supported collegiality and interaction between the teaching staff. The arrangements associated with the communal table supported not only Alice's learning, but the ongoing learning and development of all teachers.

While the regularly used communal table in Alice's teaching department was valuable in developing an in-between space that often supported the creation of a communicative learning space, the Horticulture Department's scheduled daily morning tea, discussed in Vignette 7.3, was perhaps even more supportive.

Vignette 7.3 Morning tea as support for teacher learning – Michael

Michael was a casually employed Horticulture teacher. The Horticulture Department that Michael joined had a scheduled daily morning tea. Morning tea was held around a connected group of tables in the staffroom and there was easy access to mugs, boiling water, and a refrigerator. It was not compulsory, but highly valued by teachers and attended by all.

Even though Michael was teaching only six hours a week, he tried hard to attend morning tea as often as he could, even on days when he was not teaching, because of the valuable ideas and information he encountered in the morning tea discussions. As Michael noted:

> Just to hear what they are doing. What is difficult for them. What they find nice. All their good and bad stories.

These daily morning teas provided a chance to hear stories, to ask questions, and to develop a sense of solidarity with other teachers. Michael reported several instances where there were things that he found out about during morning tea that he hadn't previously known he needed to know. These included information about teaching approaches, administrative arrangements, and relevant resources. Michael also took the opportunity to access his manager and other experienced teachers toward the end of morning tea if he had any specific questions.

So what?

In many places, daily scheduled morning teas have been removed with the view to increasing efficiency. The experiences of Michael and Ewan (see Vignette 7.7) indicate that much more is happening during morning tea than taking a break from teaching.

Not all teachers are in a position where there are colleagues from the same teaching department on the campus where they are working. Vignette 7.4 tells the story of one such teacher who was also faced with several other barriers to interacting with her colleagues.

Vignette 7.4 Casually employed full-time teacher in regional areas – Maria

Remember Maria, the casually employed teacher who taught across three regional campuses, A, B and C, where campuses A and C were about a one-hour drive in opposite directions from campus B? On two of the campuses Maria did not have any colleagues in her teaching area and on the third campus her colleague was an experienced but disgruntled teacher who threatened to retire "at any time". There were other teachers on each campus in various teaching areas but the campuses were set up in such a way that there was no easy way or place for Maria to casually interact with other teachers: the staffrooms were teaching area specific, and teachers outside those areas were not welcomed; and there were no longer any canteens or coffee shops on any of the campuses.

One of the ways that this problem of teacher isolation has been addressed is a longstanding tradition established by the library staff of a teachers' morning tea at a regular time every Friday. Maria noted:

> It doesn't matter what campus you're at, you just know that on Friday mornings, if you turn up to the library, there's going to be cheese and crackers and a cuppa.

Maria found this valuable in supporting her learning and in supporting a feeling of collegiality.

> For example, the librarian [campus B], she's been with TAFE [Technical and Further Education colleges] for over 20 years and she, oh, my goodness, she's such a wealth of knowledge, and so you just know that on Friday mornings, if you're in [campus B], you go to the library and you have a cuppa with Robyn.

Maria added:

> … and this is the exciting thing: we have staff come out of the woodwork…the automotive teachers come down, the

veterinary teachers come in, the agricultural teachers, teachers that you don't usually get to see because they run on a different schedule or because you're across a different campus, so it's really interesting, and not only that, but visiting teachers will also come in.

At these morning teas Maria has several agendas. She wants to learn what she can about various local events that might be of value for her or her students, such as professional learning sessions offered by local organisations (the example she gave was of a local charity working with people with mental health issues). She wants to meet with the teachers from other teaching areas because her students are undertaking a foundation course and she often facilitates their move to another area of study once they have developed the basic skills she is supporting them with.

It is also at these morning teas that Maria meets people who might offer her additional teaching work. She noted that the person employing her at the time of the interview was concerned that she might be "taken away" by the head of another school who she meets at morning teas.

Maria characterised it as:

> …just that little web that we weave of internal communication that is more localised than the newsletter that we get once a week which is sort of more from a corporate, strategic point of view.

So what?

There are a couple of factors to highlight here. First, the librarians very deliberately created a space for teachers to gather at a scheduled time and place. Next, Maria has been proactive in making the most of the possibilities that these gatherings provide, including seeking possibilities for her students, learning what she can from experienced teachers and the librarians, and developing increased local knowledge related to each regional area where she is working.

As Vignette 7.4 shows, while some passive learning can happen in in-between spaces, teacher agency is important and teachers can deliberately seek to learn in in-between spaces. It is not necessary to wait for an in-between space to be created by others; teachers can deliberately create such spaces.

Creating in-between spaces

Having seen the value of in-between spaces, the next step is to consider how to create such spaces. We begin with a discussion of how individual teachers can create an in-between space to support their learning (and the learning of others). Vignette 7.5 below outlines an example in which a relatively new teacher worked to create an in-between space where teachers gathered regularly.

Vignette 7.5 Friday afternoon tea – Trevor

Remember Trevor who applied for a teaching position with a teaching department that included a Head of School, permanent and casual teachers, an administrative assistant, and a technical support officer? Within six months of starting in the position there was no longer a Head of School, an administrative assistant, or a technical support officer, almost all permanently employed teachers had resigned, and the remaining casual teachers arrived to teach their classes and left immediately afterwards.

Trevor felt very isolated and tried several avenues to seek support and advice from experienced teachers and administrators. One of these was the establishment of a regular Friday afternoon tea. He invited teachers from teaching departments located nearby. He noted:

> We've started a thing on a Friday afternoon to all get together and have a hot chocolate, and this afternoon I brought in freshly cooked muffins, just to get together and talk, and that's when you pick up things. Just general conversations rather than talking seriously with them, just talk openly, like "I had this problem with this guy", "oh that guy was with me before and this is how I got round the problem, and go talk to such and such, they'll know".

So what?

In looking at Trevor's experiences of an afternoon tea just once a week compared with that of Michael (Vignette 7.3), who could have access to a daily morning tea with experienced teachers from his teaching area, Trevor did not benefit as much. However, Trevor reported that he found the chats at afternoon tea were useful in supporting his learning, and especially in giving him suggestions for who else he could contact for advice about specific things. He also valued just making a connection with other teachers. Trevor's was a relatively extreme example where he was employed to undertake both a teaching role and a qualification coordination role with no prior experience or educational qualifications related to teaching. He was also expecting (and promised) a range of technical, administrative, and teaching support, as well as relatively close supervision, and these were all removed; some before he even began work and the rest over the next six months. Creating the in-between space over afternoon tea was just one of the various approaches that Trevor used to get support, information, and guidance, as well as the fledgling development of solidarity with the other teachers.

Vignette 7.6 below provides another instance of a teacher working to create in-between spaces to support her learning. Tamsin was proactive in creating in-between spaces, and in making the most of in-between spaces created by others.

Vignette 7.6 Drop in for a cuppa; and drop in for a chat – Tamsin

Tamsin teaches a Foundation Studies course on a small campus (Regional Campus) that is an hour's drive from where she lives. She is the only person in her teaching area who works on that campus. This is the first time that a foundation course has been offered at Regional Campus, and Tamsin has an 18-month employment contract to see if there is a demand for the course. Tamsin is not very familiar with the town, and because of a range of factors including the timetabling of

Learning in in-between spaces

her teaching, she has little chance to interact with other teachers on that campus. She was given a workspace in the open-plan administration office separated from other teachers because "they didn't have anywhere else to put me". Tamsin describes her circumstances on campus as "a bit of a little isolated bubble".

Tamsin is very aware of the value of in-between spaces in supporting her learning, and she has deliberately sought out in-between spaces. This vignette outlines two unrelated in-between spaces that Tamsin has been able to create or has access to.

Many of Tamsin's students are Aboriginal people, and Regional Campus has an Aboriginal Access Centre. Shortly after Tamsin started teaching on the campus, she became aware that she needed to learn more to be able to better support the learning of her Aboriginal students. The people in the Aboriginal Access Centre were very welcoming. They have a cup of tea at 3.00 pm every day. Tamsin tries to join them for a cup of tea whenever she is on campus, partly so that she can learn more about teaching her Aboriginal students, and partly because many of her students also use the Access Centre and she and the Aboriginal Access teachers can work together to better support student learning. When Tamsin joins the Aboriginal Access Centre teachers for a cup of tea, she is quite explicit about seeking support and understanding. She notes, "I will go in and say, 'This has happened, what does that mean?' because they're a very welcoming team." She seeks to gain a greater understanding of Aboriginal culture, as well as to learn teaching approaches that better support Aboriginal students.

Another in-between space that Tamsin has created is with the Information Technology (IT) Department of the TAFE college located in her hometown (and on the campus where she used to teach before taking on her new role). Tamsin officially works four days a week at Regional Campus. On the fifth day she regularly "drops in" to chat with the IT people at "Hometown Campus" (there is no IT Department on Regional Campus). This arrangement developed over time as Tamsin regularly interacted with the people in the IT Department. Once students have completed the course with Tamsin, any further study they want to do will almost certainly need to be online, and almost all her students enter the course with no online experience or skills. There are limited computer facilities at Regional Campus and Tamsin works with the IT Department to fix old computers so they can be used by her students. In this in-between space the chat is almost always related to IT in some way but is not always work related. Tamsin gets support and advice related to computers, IT programs, and how to support her students with IT. She also shares her successes with IT-related matters and the IT Department have used some of her ideas in their work with other teaching areas.

So what?

Tamsin has made the most of the existing arrangements to support her learning. The Aboriginal Access Centre staff were welcoming and available to support Tamsin's learning. Tamsin was proactive in joining them for a cup of tea and a chat. Like Maria (Vignette 7.4), Tamsin has an agenda at tea time and during her drop-in chats with the IT Department; she wants to support her learning for the explicit purpose of supporting the learning of her students.

The examples provided in Vignettes 7.5 and 7.6 are where individual teachers have been struggling to find connection and support and were successful in doing so in in-between spaces to varying degrees. Organisations can also be proactive in creating in-between spaces. Approaches that can be implemented by organisations and local managers are brought together in the conclusion.

Increasing possibilities for in-between spaces to become communicative learning spaces

In-between spaces can be created and still not lead to learning. They could instead just be a social space where people interact, and they often are. Drawing on earlier work from Bhabha (1994), Habermas (1996), and Kemmis and McTaggert (2005), Sjolie et al. (2019) identified an in-between space where learning takes place as a *communicative learning space*. Communicative learning spaces are a "democratic, safe and supportive social space where trust is crucial" (p. 367). People are respectful of each other in communicative learning spaces, seeking intersubjective agreement and mutual understanding (Kemmis & McTaggert, 2005). Sjolie et al. considered three cases – two where communicative learning spaces were identified, and one where there was an unsuccessful attempt to create such a space. They found several factors that contributed to the creation of a communicative learning space: regularly scheduled informal or semi-formal meetings; a shared language (for instance, the language of the horticulture industry that was shared by the Horticulture teachers); and a sense of trust and solidarity between participants that was supported and developed through sharing stories. In the first two cases, the participants all spoke the same "language" – for instance, the industry language related to the trade that they were teaching. In the third case, there was no common "language" and participants did not have a common understanding of core concepts. This was further exacerbated by a lack of solidarity between participants.

While Sjolie et al. (2019) found that a shared language and scheduled meetings were valuable, in the cases where a communicative learning space was created they found that the sharing of stories and the development of trust were central aspects of the interactions. They noted "the development of solidarity and the ongoing development of trust are intertwined so that each support and furthers the other" (p. 379).

The sharing of stories can be powerful in supporting learning and can also further support the development of a sense of solidarity within the teaching team. In my research, I found the stories shared during morning tea included:

- successes with teaching and assessment
- issues that were bemusing for the teller
- ideas related to teaching or assessment approaches
- debriefing from a stressful, confusing, or difficult teaching experience
- interactions with employers
- concerns about student actions
- new products or approaches used in industry
- student successes
- problem-solving discussions.

Other research has also found that the sharing of stories and ideas supports learning. For instance, Rantalo and Karp (2018) found that sharing stories between colleagues was valuable in supporting the learning of police recruits.

They found several factors associated with this, including the development of a sense of belonging and the importance of being able to make a contribution to the team. They noted that sharing occupation-related stories with colleagues enabled the recruits to make sense of their occupational experiences, and that "stories increase knowledge of how to function in an occupational community" (p. 173). That is, sharing stories helps people learn "how to go on".

Trust has also been found to be an important factor that enables teacher learning. Edwards-Groves et al. (2016) found that the development of relational trust between teachers was powerful in facilitating their learning. In their work related to teacher learning and action research, they identified five different categories of relational trust: interpersonal, interactional, intersubjective, intellectual, and pragmatic (pp. 378–379). Francisco et al. (2021), again looking at teacher learning, found that all categories of trust needed time to develop and that interpersonal trust formed the foundation for building the other categories of trust. Sjolie et al. (2019) found that at least three of the categories of trust (and perhaps all five) identified by Edwards-Groves et al. (2016) were important in creating communicative learning spaces: interpersonal, interactive, and intersubjective.

So, what might this mean for VET and FE teachers learning in in-between spaces? Trust develops in spaces where teachers can meet often and regularly in a relatively non-formal and non-hierarchical way. Interactional trust develops through openly sharing ideas, where people listen to each other and consider alternative approaches. Solomon et al.'s (2006) example quoted earlier in this chapter about the tearoom chats where ideas and problems were shared as well as "3am thoughts … 'Guess what I thought of last night'" (p. 10), is a good example of a workplace where people felt safe to share ideas. Sjolie et al. (2019) found that where a sense of solidarity and trust existed, teachers could share alternative views and openly disagree. They noted that, in such an environment, teachers could also raise and discuss "concerns about the practices of others" (p. 377). They argue further that:

> It was with the solid basis of trust, developed over a period of time, that these alternative approaches and discussions about each-other's teaching practices were able to lead to ongoing learning and development for the teachers involved. We also suggest that to openly raise issues of conflict and discrepancies is crucial to support professional learning.
>
> (p. 377)

Learning in in-between spaces

Intersubjective trust (supported by a sense of professional equality) can be developed through engaging in shared activities. At a simple level, we can see the daily morning tea as one such shared activity. It is important also to remain aware that these interactions over morning tea do not exist in isolation. The teachers are often engaged in a range of other interactions throughout their workday (this is discussed in more detail in Chapter 5).

Intellectual trust relates to trusting colleagues' knowledge, skills, and understanding. In my research, I have found that when teachers are new to teaching, they sometimes take a while to develop intellectual trust with those teachers whose teaching areas are different to theirs. For instance, one participant was a make-up teacher and she did not have a sense of intellectual trust with the beauty therapy teachers who had not worked in the make-up industry. Over time and through ongoing interactions, most people who had regular interactions with other teachers came to value the knowledge and skills of a broader range of teachers. Unfortunately, in the case just mentioned, the environment in which this teacher worked did not enable interactions with other teachers and the intellectual trust did not develop – this negatively impacted her ongoing learning. Pragmatic trust relates to ideas and approaches being implementable.

Vignette 7.7 below provides an example of a valuable in-between space that often became a communicative learning space. I have highlighted the different categories of trust that were apparent in this site.

Vignette 7.7 Smoko – Ewan

Ewan's workplace had a morning tea (referred to by the teachers as "smoko") from 10.00–10.30 every day. Smoko was highly valued by all teachers, and teachers would always attend, even at times when they were very busy. At one smoko I attended, two teachers had a tight deadline and apologised to their colleagues that they had to work during smoko – but they did so at the end of the communal table rather than at their workstations, and occasionally joined in the discussions. Ewan was an Air Conditioning and Refrigeration teacher. Smoko was held together with the teachers from the Electrical Department. Air Conditioning and Refrigeration students also undertake some Electrical subjects as part of their trade qualification, so the teachers from each department had shared students and a shared industry language to some extent.

The daily smoko was a long-established tradition and had been taking place for as long as any of the teachers could remember. The teaching departments had recently moved to a new building and the managers of the departments had insisted that the new building had a space for smoko that included a communal table, hot water, and a sink. Both teaching departments had minimal staff turnover, so teachers had known each other for years. There was a strong sense of interpersonal trust between the teachers. There was also clear interactional trust that was strong enough to support the sharing of alternative ideas. One of the teachers (Jason) had what the others considered to be progressive ideas about electric cars. While many did not entirely share his ideas, they were interested to hear about an electric car conversion project that he was working on with his senior students. His ideas and approaches were treated with caution, but not rejected. Another teacher was considered by many of the teachers to be too traditional in his teaching approaches. They referred to him as an "old school master" and encouraged him to teach in different ways; however, they respected his industry knowledge. They deliberately worked with him in a collegial way to develop more authentic assessment methods because they felt the students (who they would encounter in other classes) would benefit. Intellectual trust was apparent in that they respected each-other's industry knowledge. This was extended to Jason's "progressive" approach that they were willing to consider.

So what?

As noted previously, all categories of trust take time to develop. This includes elapsed time as well as actual time spent in each-other's company. These longstanding daily smokos provided that time.

As Sjolie et al. (2019) note:

> It is likely that the development of a communicative learning space – a democratic, safe and supportive social space where trust is crucial – is supportive of professional learning across a range of professions. It is, however, important to emphasise that a communicative learning space is not always harmonious; it is not idyllic, and it is not ideal. It is always contested, and the important thing is to create the conditions of solidarity under which contestation is possible.
>
> (p. 379)

The daily smoko that the Air Conditioning and Refrigeration and the Electrical teaching teams attended created such a space.

The fragility of communicative learning spaces

Communicative learning spaces are valuable in supporting teacher learning. However, it is important to note that these spaces are fragile.

Solomon et al. (2006) found that VET teachers were sometimes displeased when the researchers identified the lunchroom as a space where learning happened. They noted in one instance, "It appeared that the teacher regarded the naming of the lunchroom as a learning space as transgressive. He could admit that learning occurred, but to formally acknowledge it as a learning space was to intrude into a protected environment" (p. 9). In a sense this was their personal space that should not be encroached on.

In a later paper, Boud et al. (2009) focussed on workplace interventions by managers that were deliberately set up to increase productivity by using informal learning arrangements. They considered two interventions where an organisation deliberately focussed on something that was taking place informally and formalised it – one was a morning tea, and the other was something that the organisation called "toolbox talks", which was essentially a deliberate setting up of work-related chats between colleagues together with their manager. Regular, compulsory morning teas were established where staff were required to report back on their learning. This might be learning due to attending a course, or learning through work. When morning tea was deliberately structured as a learning space, the opposite happened. Boud et al. (2009) reported that, "(B)y requiring workers to chat at particular times, the workers have been rendered inarticulate: 'we just stand around and stare at each other', 'people don't talk like they used to'" (p. 332).

In one of the cases that they considered, Sjolie et al. (2019) found that a communicative learning space was not created, even though there had been an intention to do so. They suggest that part of the reason for this was that what did develop was a "performance space". A performance space is where participants must "perform" rather than chat and interact as they choose without fear of surveillance. With the workplace interventions described by Boud et al. (2009), not only was there an attempt to formalise the learning that had previously occurred during morning tea, they also created a performance space when they required people to give a presentation about learning that they had undertaken elsewhere. The previously personal space had been overtaken by "the system", and by formalising the in-between space they "broke" the fragile communicative learning space that had been created between colleagues. A similar thing can be seen to have happened with the toolbox talks.

With the toolbox talks, staff were required to attend a meeting to "chat" about their work and to "diarise" their learning through these chats. Boud et al. (2009) found that these interventions were often resented by the people they were set up for, and that "by imposing and thus formalising chat, the nature and value of chat changes when chat is made compulsory and when chatter comes under surveillance" (p. 331). Again, personal chat was taken over by the system and the space that was previously a communicative learning space was reshaped into something else. Boud et al. note, "While it may be possible to foster everyday chat we need to recognise that by taking up talk for learning purposes we may work against or inhibit its positive benefits. Resistance can be mobilised" (p. 332). They argue that "informal learning and everyday chat at work are ... vital, but by naming and managing them as learning, the meanings and experiences change. From governing themselves, workers experience being governed by others" (p. 332).

It becomes apparent then that supporting the creation of a communicative learning space needs to be done with care. A deliberate attempt to create a communicative learning space might have the opposite effect. As we saw in some of the Boud et al. (2009) research, it might be that it is the creation of in-between spaces that is possible, and this can set up the possibility (but not the certainty) of the creation of a communicative learning space. In a sense, then, what can be created are possibilities, not certainties. The Horticulture Department's morning tea (Vignette 7.3) and the Air Conditioning and Refrigeration Department's morning tea (Vignette 7.7) are good examples of a structure being created. Management ensured that a daily morning tea was scheduled, they ensured that a space was available in the staffroom (some other departments in the same organisation had replaced the lunchroom/tearoom with offices), and that a communal table (as well as hot water and a sink) was provided. Importantly, there was no obligation to attend, and no scheduling of particular activities or surveillance during this time.

Having seen some of the dangers of formalising informal arrangements, it is useful also to consider how formal or semi-formal arrangements might serve to support the creation of communicative learning spaces. Vignette 7.8 below tells the story of the creation of an in-between space that developed as a result of the scheduling of a regular formal staff meeting.

Vignette 7.8 In-between space after formal meeting – Tamsin

In Vignette 7.6, two in-between spaces that Tamsin accessed are outlined. Tamsin also had access to a third in-between space, and this was associated with a regular fortnightly formal online meeting. Tamsin's teaching department is spread across an entire Australian state, and most of the teachers teach in small regional areas. The coordinator had organised a fortnightly online meeting and this had been in place for some time before Tamsin joined the teaching team (this is also discussed in Chapter 5). This staff meeting was set up to allow regular communication with and between the teachers. Tamsin reported that the beginning of these meetings was usually focussed on compliance and other administrative-type matters – "everyone catches up on policies and procedures, as you do". The Head of School attends the first part of the meeting to "talk about all the new updates and things we need to be aware of" and then, when the Head of School leaves, "we all just share information of how we're going, what we've run in our classes (because we all run the same topics), the different ways in which we deliver those topics, we share that sort of information". The widely dispersed group of teachers had developed a sense of solidarity

Learning in in-between spaces

and this had already been developed before Tamsin's arrival. Tamsin was welcomed as a colleague and her university qualifications in the teaching area were valued. Tamsin identified this as one of the in-between spaces that supported her learning.

So what?

This vignette shows that a communicative learning space could be created between people who rarely, if ever, met each other face-to-face. Even more surprising is that the catalyst for developing the communicative learning space was a scheduled, compulsory, formal meeting. It is useful to consider how the meetings that Tamsin valued were different to the morning tea personal development (PD) sessions discussed by Solomon et al. (2006) that teachers resented and that did not result in the development of in-between spaces.

One important difference was that the meeting did not replace an existing informal arrangement. Additionally, the teachers were relatively isolated, and this provided an opportunity to connect with their colleagues that was not otherwise available. The fact that the Head of School was an invited guest who attended for a specific purpose and then left to some extent characterised the meeting as belonging to the teachers and not to "management".

The shared discipline, knowledge, and language are also likely to have been valuable, particularly as the teachers were often the only people from their teaching area (Foundation Skills) on each of the campuses where they worked. This shared language was valued even more because it was not part of their day-to-day experiences.

The meetings had been happening for some time when Tamsin joined the team, and so there had been time to develop some level of trust between colleagues. Tamsin spoke only of the sharing of success stories during the semi-formal part of the meeting; however, she reports asking for advice, ideas, and support with problem solving during the final "chatting" part of the meeting (see Chapter 5). Some of the approaches that she learnt during this time were quite innovative and focussed on the particular cohort of students that the team was working with. This willingness to be vulnerable, and to seek support, shows the development of interactional trust to some extent.

It is important to be cautious about the example in Vignette 7.8. This was the only instance in my research over a number of years and a number of organisations where formal arrangements have supported the development of an in-between space (apart from those that are in-between formal arrangements such as morning tea and lunch during a training course). It is included to show that it is possible, not to suggest that it is commonplace.

Creating in-between spaces that support the development of a communicative learning space is complex and needs to be handled delicately.

Conclusion and summary

In-between spaces that enable informal interaction between colleagues at work can be valuable for supporting teacher learning. This chapter has outlined the concept of in-between spaces (spaces that are in various ways in-between the professional and personal) and argued that it is not enough to have in-between spaces – arrangements need to be in place so that in-between spaces can become communicative learning spaces. A communicative learning space is democratic, respectful, and safe. Key characteristics that support the development of communicative learning spaces are a shared language (such as the language of the trade that all are teaching), the sharing of stories, trust, and solidarity.

Arrangements that can support the development of an in-between space include a communal table, a scheduled, non-compulsory and informal meeting time (such as morning tea), and access to an informal meeting place such as a tearoom. Communicative learning spaces are fragile, and efforts to formalise them usually end in extinguishing them. Similarly, surveillance of in-between spaces can lead to their demise, or lead to them being moved elsewhere.

Creating an in-between space that becomes a communicative learning space can be of benefit to organisations and individuals. Organisations can foster the conditions that can lead to a communicative learning space and avoid trying to control such spaces. Trust and solidarity build over time and with ongoing and regular interactions. They cannot be forced, only invitational.

Questions to consider

For the individual

- What in-between spaces are available for you at your workplace (or associated with your work)?
  - What could you do to increase the chances of these becoming communicative learning spaces?
- What possibilities exist for you to create an in-between space that would support the learning of you and your colleagues? Who might support you with this?

For the organisation

- Can you identify arrangements that result in limiting in-between spaces in the workplace?
  - What changes might be made to remove these limitations?
- What arrangements can be made in the short term to create the environment for an in-between space?
- What longer-term arrangements could be made?

References

Bhabha, H. K. (1994). *The location of culture*. London: Routledge.

Boud, D., Rooney, D., & Solomon, N. (2009). Talking up learning at work: cautionary tales in co-opting everyday learning. *International Journal of Lifelong Education, 28*(3), 325–336.

Edwards-Groves, C., Grootenboer, P., & Ronnerman, K. (2016). Facilitating a culture of relational trust in school-based action research: recognising the role of middle leaders. *Educational Action Research, 24*(3), 369–386. doi: 10.1080/09650792.2015.1131175

Francisco, S., Forssten Seiser, A., & Grice, C. (2021). Professional learning that enables the development of critical praxis. *Professional Development in Education*, 1–15. doi:10.1080/19415257.2021.1879228

Habermas, J. (1996). *Between facts and norms. Contributions to a discourse theory of law and democracy* (W. Rehg, Trans.). Malden, MA: MIT Press.

Kemmis, S. & McTaggert, R. (2005). Participatory action research: communicative action and the public sphere. In *The Sage handbook of qualitative research*, edited by N. K. Denzin & Y. S. Lincoln. Thousand Oaks, CA: Sage, pp. 559–603.

Rantalo, O. & Karp, S. (2018). Stories of policing: the role of storytelling in police students' sensemaking of early work-based experiences. *Vocations and Learning*, *11*(1), 161–177.

Sjolie, E., Francisco, S., & Langelotz, L. (2019). Communicative learning spaces and learning to become a teacher. *Pedagogy, Culture and Society*, *27*(3), 365–382.

Solomon, N., Boud. D., & Rooney, D. (2006). The in-between: exposing everyday learning at work. *International Journal of Lifelong Education*, *25*(1), 3–13.

8

Leading learning
Building a trellis of practices to support professional learning

This chapter focusses on leading the workplace learning of Vocational Education and Training (VET) and Further Education (FE) teachers. It begins by considering the concept of leading more broadly. Establishing a trellis of practices that support learning (PSLs) in the teaching workplace is then discussed. Action research is identified as one possible approach for making appropriate changes. The chapter includes a section focussing on casual teachers, and one focussing on accomplished teachers (acknowledging that casual teachers can also be accomplished teachers). Two related matters are also addressed in this chapter – teacher agency and reflective practice. The chapter ends with questions to consider when establishing a trellis of PSLs in your workplace. We begin by examining the notion of "leading learning".

The chapter draws on ideas and strategies introduced in earlier chapters; while all chapters are relevant, this chapter mainly draws on Chapter 4 (which uses the theory of practice architectures to explore the site-based arrangements that enable and constrain teacher learning), Chapter 5 (which outlines the development of a trellis of practices that support learning [PSLs]), and Chapter 7 (which considers the learning that happens in in-between spaces). You will get more from this chapter if you have read these chapters first.

Leading learning[1]

Leading is an important component of successful change and development – for organisations and individuals. There has been much research

---

1 If you want to get into the specifics before reading this section, skip to the section *Trellis of Practices that Support Learnings*. If you do that, I recommend that you return to this section afterwards because it contains some useful underpinning ideas.

DOI: 10.4324/9781003112624-8

into leadership and leading and, over time, leadership research and related advice for leaders in organisations have changed. This is not the place for a history of leadership studies; suffice it to say that the previous focus on the charismatic individual leader pushing through *his* preconceived agenda is now understood to limit the development of more successful outcomes (see for instance, Wilkinson 2022; Wilkinson & Kemmis, 2015). Such a focus neglects, among other things, the important influence of context on what happens and how it happens.

More contemporary understandings include a focus on the practices of leading rather than on the leader. Using the theory of practice architectures (see Chapter 4), we can understand leading as being shaped by the practice architectures (the cultural-discursive, material-economic, and social-political arrangements) that exist in, or are brought into, a site. The practices involved in leading, and the people who engage in these practices, are influenced by the practice architectures in the local site. Interestingly, by engaging in leading practices, people can make changes to the practice architectures of a site. So, for instance, a Head of School (who has positional power because of their role) who develops the agenda for a staff meeting can arrange the agenda so that others can engage in leading practices during the meeting. As Edwards-Groves et al. (2020) argue, "Leading as a practice may have as its central project … the enabling, transforming, or reorienting [of] other practices, or the creation of conditions conducive to such change" (p. 122).

By focussing on practices of leading, and the practice architectures that enable and constrain learning practices, we can envisage leading as working to make changes to existing conditions to enable new practices (Wilkinson et al., 2010). The discussion of "power over", "power through" and "power with" (Smeed et al., 2009) in Chapter 4 is worth revisiting in relation to the concept of leading learning. To quickly recap, "power with" involves working together in a collegial, non-hierarchical, and collaborative way. "Power through" involves using positional power to arrange positive outcomes for others, such as arranging possibilities for team teaching. To successfully lead learning, a focus on achieving power with, or at least power through, is crucial. But what might this look like in your local site? At a broad level it includes enabling teacher agency (more on this later).

An important consideration with leading learning is who does the leading. In recent times, for many VET organisations, the role of the Head of School (of course, there are various titles associated with this role, but we will use this one here) has needed to prioritise business activities, leaving little time/space available for a focus on teaching and learning. While, in many organisations, leading the learning of teachers is also identified as the role of the person holding that position, day-to-day reality often means that there is limited time available to undertake that part of the role. Some organisations have a Senior Teacher role (again, with a range of titles). People in this role are teachers who are given some teaching release hours to undertake work that includes supporting teacher development. Grootenboer et al. (2014) refer to these people as "middle leaders". They identify middle leaders as having:

> ...some positional (and/or acknowledged) responsibility to bring about change in their schools, yet maintain close connections to the classroom as sites where student learning occurs. In one sense middle leaders bridge the educational work of classrooms and the management practices of the administrators/leaders.
>
> (p. 509)

In VET and FE, it is often middle leaders who can engage in leading practices related to teacher learning and work with teachers to make changes in the workplace. Interestingly, these people also often have an important mentoring role.

Leading teacher learning can involve many and various practices. At a broad level, it can involve making learning opportunities available and creating conditions where learning opportunities can be taken up. While the ongoing registration of a Registered Training Organisation (RTO) in Australia requires teachers to undertake professional development each year, many of my research participants have suggested that this is often a "tick and flick" exercise in their organisations and can sometimes involve relatively limited learning. Some of these same participants have then gone on to identify the (often extensive) learning that they have done through such activities as informal mentoring (as both mentors and mentees) and other activities that make up a trellis of PSLs in their workplace (outlined in Chapter 5). Working to support the development of a trellis of PSLs can be a powerful and effective way to lead learning.

Enabling teacher agency

Much of this book highlights site-based conditions that enable and constrain teacher learning. However, as noted in Chapter 4, individuals can, and do, make a difference. We have established that what teachers do, and how they do it, can be constrained or enabled by the practice architectures in a site. At the same time, practices "are conducted, reproduced, and transformed by the individuals who inhabit them, who come to embody and realise them in their day to day actions" (Kemmis et al., 2017, p. 249). Similarly, the conditions in a site are largely created by people, and people can change these same conditions.

Positional leaders (those who are given a clear and mandated leading role), middle leaders, and groups of teachers working collaboratively are especially able to make changes to existing conditions. The site-based arrangements that enable and constrain teacher learning are an example of conditions that can be changed. As Olin et al. (2020) argue, "Professional learning that is worthwhile for educators, students and society as a whole emerges when teachers have agency to act and when this action takes into account teachers' professional experience, competencies, values and ethics" (p. 155). Working to enable teacher agency is an important aspect of leading teacher learning.

Trellis of practices that support learning (PSLs)

Before you can begin to establish (or further develop) a trellis of PSLs (see Chapter 5 for information about what this is), it is helpful to consider the following questions.

- What might a trellis of PSLs look like in your local site?
- What PSLs are already in your site?
    - Who has easy access to these?
    - Whose access to these is constrained as a result of existing practice architectures?
    - Whose access to these is enabled as a result of existing practice architectures?
- How might a trellis of PSLs be established (or further developed) in your local site?

Building a trellis of PSLs is site-specific. A trellis of PSLs cannot be transferred unchanged from one site to another. As teachers, we know that a teaching approach that works well in one context may not work well in

Leading learning

another. Similarly, some PSLs that interact well in one context may not interact elsewhere. A trellis of PSLs creates a niche that supports teacher learning (the same is true for the learning of other workers, but here we focus on teachers).

Chapter 5 provides various examples of a trellis of PSLs. In each example the trellis included a mentor. A well-trained mentor from the same local site can be a linchpin for establishing a trellis of PSLs, especially for new and casual teachers. Mentors outside the site are also valuable (especially for experienced teachers), but a mentor within the site is more likely to support the development of a trellis of PSLs, especially if they are aware of what a trellis of PSLs might include. Site-based mentors are more aware of local possibilities, and likely to be more readily available. For instance, a site-based mentor is more likely to be aware of local matters such as what took place in the staff meeting yesterday, and who is likely to work well together in a team-teaching arrangement. They are also more likely to be able to invite their mentee to team teach with them, or to be co-teachers with them, to discuss teaching and assessment-related matters during (or just after) morning tea, and to enable the co-development of resources, as well as teaching and assessment approaches.

A strong trellis of PSLs consists of various arrangements. As Chapter 7 shows, in-between spaces that become communicative learning spaces can be valuable in supporting teacher learning. Other components of a strong trellis of PSLs (see Chapter 5) include arrangements that enable:

- observation – observing others; being observed
  - observation of teaching (for instance, mentors observing teachers, teachers observing mentors and other teachers) and associated feedback
  - observation of out-of-class practices (for instance, course development, lesson planning and preparation, contributing to meetings)
- communicative learning spaces (for instance, sometimes found around a communal staffroom table)
- co-development of resources
- teacher access to in-between spaces.

Are these practices enabled in your workplace? What changes might be made to enable the development of a trellis of PSLs? Table 8.3 at the end of this chapter provides some questions for you to consider as part of a site survey that will help you answer this question. You will note that the site survey has a focus on the learning of new and casually employed teachers. These PSLs are also likely to support the learning of experienced teachers to some extent. But a deliberate focus on leading the learning of experienced teachers is also valuable. There is a section on leading the learning of this group of teachers later in this chapter.

Once you have determined what already exists in the site, the next step is to determine:

- What can be changed in the short term to create more inter-related PSLs.
- What can be changed in the medium to long term to create more inter-related PSLs.

Changing the practice architectures of a site

When identifying the changes you are planning to make (short-term, medium-term and long-term), it is helpful to focus on the practice architectures from the cultural-discursive, material-economic, and social-political dimensions (see Chapter 4). It is by making changes to these arrangements that actions change – the sayings, influenced by the cultural-discursive arrangements; the doings, influenced by the material-economic arrangements; and the relatings, influenced by the social-political arrangements.

Successful change usually involves voluntary and active participation by some of those directly impacted by the changes. Passive resistance can be powerful in ensuring proposed changes are not successful. But a voluntary commitment to ongoing development can be even more powerful. It can also be valuable for a change project to be sponsored by someone in senior management. Such sponsorship can also better enable access to funds, teacher release time, support of the broader senior management team (where applicable), and smooth unexpected difficulties. Determining who you might seek such sponsorship from involves considerations such as who is likely to be interested and supportive and the pre-existing organisational hierarchies that are in place.

Communication is crucial to successful change. It is important that communication is clear, regular, and includes all people involved or who think they could be involved. If this includes more than about ten people, or if it includes some people who might not be closely involved in decision making, it can be valuable to develop a communication plan. Such a plan might include updates at staff meetings, regular (weekly, fortnightly) emails that are kept short so that people read them, and specific communication with casually employed teachers. It is also important to ensure clear communication with more senior managers, and especially the manager sponsoring the changes.

Once the team of active participants has surveyed your site, how might you go about making changes? As Spedding (2020) argues, "what might appear to be 'quick fixes' rarely, if ever, 'fix' anything and never very 'quickly'" (p. 188). Making changes that are well supported by participants and that are sustainable requires careful consideration. One approach for implementing such change is action research. Spedding notes that, "When opportunities are present for teachers to think carefully, to share their thinking with others and to improve their practice in a spirit of critical professional friendship, then meaningful change will happen" (p. 196). Action research can provide such opportunities.

Action research

Action research is an approach used by teachers (and many other practitioners) to make improvements and create sustained transformations in what happens and how it happens. For teachers, action research is usually an approach that fits well within their customary approach. As Spedding (2020) argues, "most complex practice (such as teaching) involves 'research', in the broadest sense, most of the time, as teachers are always in effect testing and renewing their expertise in contexts which are never quite the same" (p. 195). An action research project can be a valuable approach to establishing or further developing a trellis of PSLs at a local site.

Action research involves the following four phases:

Plan > Act > Observe > Reflect

These phases are undertaken in a series of cycles. One of the benefits of action research is that there is no expectation that everything will be entirely successful as soon as it is put in place. After the first cycle, the information collected is used to re-plan for the next cycle. Below is a brief overview of each of the phases of an action research cycle.

Plan

During this phase, the action research team (more about this later) considers the problem or issue and develops a plan to address it. So, after doing a survey of the PSLs in the local site (see Table 8.3), the team might begin by identifying the first set of changes that they want to make.

Act

The changes are put into place. The team needs to determine the timeframe for this phase. Depending on the changes made, it might be as little as four weeks or as long as a semester.

Observe

This phase takes place during the Act phase, and/or shortly after that. It involves collecting data about the impact of the changes made.

Reflect

During this phase, the action research team analyses the data they've collected and reflects on the outcomes.

Plan

The cycle begins again, informed by the findings from the first cycle.

The action research team

The action research team will work together through the phases of the project. A successful action research project usually involves a committed team of colleagues interested in working together to make changes in their local site. The number of people in a team varies but is usually more than two and less than eight (my preference is for a team of four to six people). If the team becomes too large, some separate teams can be established. These teams will need to communicate regularly with each other, especially if addressing the same problem or broad issue.

Leading learning

The establishment of an action research team is an important element of an action research approach. An action research team needs to be made up of people who:

- are interested in the problem/issue to be addressed and want to make improvements;
- have volunteered to be involved;
- are willing and able to give time and energy to the project.

People in an action research team should be closely involved with the practices they are trying to change. Action research is about people working together to make positive changes to their practices and sites. Some action research teams are also guided by academics/experienced researchers who can support the team by providing relevant resources and assistance related to undertaking the project. This might include data collection and data analysis techniques, recommendation of relevant literature, and suggestions and guidance related to specific approaches during each of the phases.

There is a lot of literature available about action research, and a simple web search will give you more information. If you decide to proceed with an action research approach, I recommend *The Action Research Planner: Doing critical participatory action research*, written by Kemmis et al. (2014). This book provides a good guide to planning and undertaking action research. It includes a range of resources, detailed examples of action research projects, and suggests approaches for establishing an action research team.

Where possible it is helpful for an action research project to aim to make changes in each of the three dimensions: cultural-discursive, material-economic, and social-political. The very act of forming an action research team is likely to impact on the social-political dimension. If the team is aware of the importance of the cultural-discursive arrangements, they can begin to make changes in this dimension by considering the language they use related to teacher learning. It is also worth considering the use of education and training language as well as the use of industry-related language in the teaching workplace.

Leading the learning of casually employed teachers

In Australia, a high proportion of VET teachers are employed on a casual basis – an average of 32% across all provider types, and 51% overall in TAFE colleges (Knight et al., 2020). Some individual organisations have an even higher level of casualisation. In some ways the employment of casual teachers can be seen as a risk for an organisation. This risk can be lessened where casual teachers are deliberately well supported in their learning. One of the key findings from the research into the VET workforce undertaken by Knight et al. was that "This casualisation of trainer/assessor employment may restrict opportunities to develop teaching and assessment ability with potential impacts on the quality of training delivery. This suggests there may be a need to identify appropriate ways of enabling adequate professional development for casual and other non-permanent employees" (p. 8). Students, employers, and the community expect competent and skilled VET provision. To enable this, we need to support the development of good teaching and assessment skills of all teachers, including those employed casually.

As noted in previous chapters, research shows that casual teachers usually have less access to support from colleagues as well as less access to professional development. In leading the learning of VET and FE teachers it is important to consider the needs and circumstances of casually employed teachers. Using the theory of practice architectures (see Chapter 4) can support such a deliberate focus – ensuring that the cultural-discursive arrangements (which influence the sayings in the site), material-economic arrangements (which influence the doings in the site), and social-political arrangements (which influence the relatings in the site) are deliberately supportive of casual teachers.

In other writing (Francisco, 2020), I have identified casually employed teachers as Fringe Teachers and Favela Teachers. Fringe Teachers are those employed on a casual basis to teach up to eight hours a week. Favela Teachers are employed on a casual basis and teach more than eight hours a week, and sometimes undertake more than the teaching load of a full-time teacher. The term "favela" comes from the under-resourced urban communities that have developed in some cities in Brazil. People living in favelas do not usually have access to basic services that the rest of society have. Like people living in favelas, some casually employed teachers do not have easy access to services and conditions available to others (see for instance, Sarah's Vignette 2.10 in Chapter 2). Favela Teachers, employed on an hourly basis, often work more hours than they are paid for so that they can come to know what they need to know to teach effectively. They also experience a lack of security of tenure, nonpayment during the non-teaching periods, no annual leave, no sick leave provisions, and no long-service leave. Their access to professional development is also often limited compared to their permanently employed colleagues.

Of all teachers, Fringe Teachers usually have the least access to workplace learning and other options for learning about teaching. Interestingly, in research that I undertook with novice teachers, I found that Fringe Teachers seemed to gain the least (compared with all other groups of teachers) from undertaking the required teaching qualification (the Certificate IV in Training and Assessment). This likely is because they did not have the chance to take their learning further through things such as:

- discussing their learning with colleagues
- hearing others discuss their teaching experiences and compare this with what they learnt in the course
- trialling approaches they learnt about and getting feedback from colleagues.

In this research, Fringe Teachers most often encountered arrangements that decreased their chances of having their learning supported. They often had limited access to advice and support from colleagues and managers (even less than Favela Teachers), and they were usually physically separated from other teachers in the staffroom. This lack of access to support for their learning can result in mistakes being made. For instance, in one case from my research, a Fringe Teacher taught the wrong competencies for the first four weeks of a 12-week course.

Any work to increase the learning of Fringe Teachers can usefully begin by increasing access to the support of accomplished teachers. As noted in Chapter 1, an accomplished teacher is always an experienced teacher, but an experienced teacher is not always an accomplished teacher. Years of teaching is not enough to become accomplished. Opportunities and a willingness to be involved in ongoing professional learning and developing through professional engagement are also part of being an accomplished teacher. One important component of providing better support for the learning of Fringe and Favela Teachers is acknowledging the voluntary nature of much of the ad hoc support that casual teachers receive and arranging for accomplished teachers to be given release time to provide this support.

The practice architectures that enable and constrain Fringe and Favela Teacher learning can be explored across the three dimensions: the cultural-discursive, the material-economic, and the social-political. This includes using, and importantly understanding, vocational education and training-related language, the placement of workstations, and how Fringe Teachers are welcomed (or not) into teaching discussions. In my research, Fringe Teachers and some of the Favela Teachers had less access to language related to Vocational Education and Training (VET). Learning VET language (and associated concepts) can often be like learning a foreign language – and, as we know, learning a foreign language requires regular interaction with the language in use. In one instance, after about six months, the permanent teacher who was co-teaching with a Fringe Teacher, and who was supporting her learning, assumed that the Fringe Teacher now understood the VET language commonly used in the teaching department. The Fringe Teacher was too embarrassed to seek clarification when she didn't understand and made some mistakes as a result. These mistakes negatively impacted the learning of her students. Having an awareness of this issue can be of value in supporting new and casual teachers.

When teachers are first employed, the permanent teachers they work with often remember to explain VET language (in Australia this includes terms such as "competency" and "training package") but cease doing so after a few months. Within this timeframe, most contract and permanent teachers and many Favela Teachers can learn the new language. However, this is not the case with Fringe Teachers who usually have limited opportunities to engage with the new words and their associated concepts. A more deliberate approach to accomplished teachers supporting casual teachers can be valuable.

Table 8.1 outlines some approaches that have resulted in support for casual teacher learning. While no strategy is likely to be universally successful, I have witnessed the success of these strategies in real situations. You will see that many of these strategies relate to increased access to advice and support from colleagues.

Leading learning

Table 8.1 Deliberately supporting casual teacher learning

Broad strategy	Further information	Comments
Provision of well-designed existing resources*	Give to new and casual teachers Discuss how each can be used (even if it seems obvious to you) Revisit again to ensure understanding and willingness to use the resource • discuss suitable alternatives if needed	Casual teachers (and especially Fringe Teachers) will often not use the provided resources if they do not understand how to use them, or if they are different to what they are accustomed to. Fringe Teachers are less likely to seek advice about how to use provided resources, and to instead use other resources they have accessed elsewhere. Online meetings might sometimes be a better alternative for some casual teachers.
Mentoring	Training for mentors Regular meetings. Ideally at least weekly initially • meeting to be rescheduled by mentor if not attended	A mentor who is aware of the phases of a mentoring programme, the need to ensure mentees understand VET language, and who are genuinely interested in supporting the learning of others can make a real difference to teachers' learning. See Chapters 5 and 6. Mentees are often reluctant to impose on mentors, so often do not ask questions as needed. Mentees are less likely to reschedule if a meeting is missed – often because they believe their mentor is too busy and not wishing to impose on them.

Table 8.1 (Cont.)

Broad strategy	Further information	Comments
Workstations and access to other teachers**	Include casual teachers in the same physical space as experienced teachers Establish other arrangements for easy access (such as below)	
Invite all teachers to a daily scheduled morning tea	Invite casual teachers individually by name	Because many casual teachers often miss out on communications sent to all staff (for various reasons including being left off mailing lists, not thinking they apply to them, or not finding the time to read them), it is useful to explicitly invite each individual so that they know that they are welcome (but not required) to attend.
Communication about available professional learning	Explicit and deliberate communication with Fringe and Favela Teachers about the availability of professional development opportunities is important. This might include emails to casual teachers and their mentors, hard copy information available in the tearoom, and sharing of information at staff meetings.	Fringe and Favela Teachers often do not know that professional learning opportunities are available, which essentially means that they are not available to them.

(continued)

Table 8.1 (Cont.)

Broad strategy	Further information	Comments
Make casual teachers welcome at staff meetings	Where possible, also pay for attendance at a nominated number of staff meetings a semester.	Being part of staff meetings can help casual teachers to become aware of a range of factors, including: • support that is available • available professional learning • discussions with experienced teachers before and after the meeting.
Team teaching	Team teaching can be seen as a risk management strategy when casualisation is high.	See also Table 8.2. As noted elsewhere, team teaching combines many PSLs.

* One of the practices that usually supports novice teacher learning is the provision, and use, of well-designed teaching and assessment resources. This is especially important for Fringe Teachers. However, in my research, I found that Fringe Teachers made less use of pre-existing resources than any other teachers. When a teacher was permanently employed or on contract, if they did not believe a provided resource was appropriate, or did not understand how to use it, they would discuss it with their manager or an experienced teacher. When Fringe Teachers encountered such resources, they mostly rejected them without seeking further information and replaced the resource with something else (perhaps from their training many years previously). In some instances, this resulted in students using outdated and even incorrect resources.

** In my research, most casual teachers were physically separated from experienced teachers. This is perhaps due to the experienced teachers' desire to decrease ad hoc questions and requests for support. Other arrangements can be put in place to address this issue. Such arrangements might include:
- some accomplished teachers being given a clear role to support new and casual teachers, with associated teaching hour reductions
- setting up the staffroom in such a way that new and casual teachers have easy access to the accomplished teachers who have responsibility for supporting them.

Leading the learning of experienced and accomplished teachers

In exploring the professional development of VET teachers, Dymock and Tyler (2018) considered the expectations and requirements for ongoing learning in four other professional areas: health, accounting, law, and school education. They found that each of these four professions had specific annual requirements for ongoing professional development and expectations for continuous learning throughout a worker's career. Dymock and Tyler argue that:

> ... professions are characterised by a calling, an understanding of the theoretical, the exercising of judgement in uncertain conditions, learning from experience, and the monitoring of quality and the aggregating of knowledge within a community. If VET practitioners were able to see themselves in those terms, the status of VET in Australia would be transformed.
>
> (p. 209)

Like other professions, teachers need regular professional learning throughout their careers (if you are reading this book this is not new information for you). This professional learning needs to meet individual as well as personal needs. There has been extensive research to show that one-off professional development sessions rarely make any difference to what people do and how they do it. Professional learning needs to be ongoing, sustained over time, and acted on in practice (Olin et al., 2020).

In my research, I found that some teaching areas supported experienced teachers to further develop their learning by undertaking higher-level teaching qualifications. In some of the sites where I undertook research, teachers had completed or were undertaking bachelor- or graduate-level teaching qualifications (see Vignette 8.1 as an example). Smith et al. (2015) found that undertaking a university-level teaching qualification increased the skills of VET teachers in six main areas, including their skills related to teaching, writing, and ICT. It also resulted in more developed personal skills, greater VET-sector related skills, and improved general business and industry-related skills. This included:

> ... in terms of VET-sector specific knowledge ... VET curriculum practices, general VET sector knowledge such as "working more effectively with industry", and VET specific language, literacy and numeracy issues. Pedagogical skills included delivery skills, capacity to improve teaching practice, assessment and understanding learners.
>
> (p. 6)

It is unlikely that it is a coincidence that I found greater support for the learning of all teachers in the workplace in those teaching areas where a higher proportion of teachers had a university-level teaching qualification. Experienced teachers can have a positive influence on the learning of their colleagues through their ongoing learning, through providing a role model, sharing what they are learning, by creating an expectation of ongoing teacher learning, and even through the language that they use.

> ## Vignette 8.1 The Air Conditioning and Refrigeration Department
>
> In the Air Conditioning and Refrigeration teaching team, more than half of the teachers, as well as the Head of School, have, or are currently studying for, a bachelor- or graduate-level teaching qualification. This is also the case for the team of Electrical teachers in the same staffroom and with whom they interact during smoko (morning tea) each day. The language used, and the ideas raised, when discussing teaching and assessment was clearly influenced by this. As you will have seen in other chapters, this teaching department provided a strong trellis of PSLs.

In exploring the practice architectures that enable and constrain teacher learning, it is also helpful to consider, in relation to your teaching department:

- What teaching qualifications are teachers expected to have when they are first employed as teachers?
- What teaching qualifications are experienced teachers expected to have?

- How many teachers have higher-level teaching qualifications?
  - What arrangements are made to share the learning from this study?
  - Could this be improved? How?
- How are teachers supported to undertake higher-level qualifications?
- What positive impact do these teachers have on the learning of other teachers (note, this might be subtle rather than overt)?

This book is about supporting the workplace learning of teachers, so the questions in Table 8.3 focus on the workplace. However, for experienced teachers (and novice teachers in some instances), input from outside the workplace can be valuable. Some strategies for supporting the learning of experienced teachers are included in Table 8.2. The strategies in Tables 8.1 and 8.2 are not intended to be exhaustive, but they do provide a useful starting point. There are, of course, other useful strategies that can be put in place to support teacher learning in the workplace. In implementing these strategies, it is also useful to consider how they might be included in a trellis of PSLs rather than just as stand-alone PSLs.

Table 8.2 Deliberately supporting experienced teacher learning

Broad strategy	Further information	Comments
Support for experienced teachers to become mentors	Mentors often report as much learning from mentoring as mentees do.	Establishing a mentoring programme (including training and support for mentors) across the organisation or within the local site can be valuable. See Chapter 6 for more information about mentoring.
Guest speakers	Industry guest speakers support student learning as well as teacher learning. Inviting people who do research in your teaching area or research into VET or FE teaching more broadly, can be valuable.	Most people who are invited to speak with students and/or teachers are happy and willing to do so. Researchers are often keen to share the outcomes of their research with people who are interested.

(*continued*)

Leading learning

Table 8.2 (Cont.)

Broad strategy	Further information	Comments
Networking opportunities	Strategies might include: • joining professional, industry, and education networks and groups (local and national) • attending conferences • deliberately seeking invitations to other VET organisations to see what they are doing • being willing for teachers from other organisations (or other sites from the same organisation) to visit your campus, and to engage in discussions with teachers.	Useful to ask teachers who engage in networking opportunities to share their learning with the rest of the team from time to time.
Scheduled regular (ideally daily) morning tea		This is included in the table for casual teachers. It is equally valuable for experienced teachers.
Team teaching	Team teaching with a trusted colleague. Beginning with a clear understanding that each person will seek to learn from the other, and that both will seek to learn together. Works best where there is joint development of teaching approaches, assessment tasks, and teaching resources.	Experienced teachers can benefit from team teaching with a trusted colleague. This can include reflecting together pre- and post-teaching.

Table 8.2 (Cont.)

Broad strategy	Further information	Comments
Deliberately contacting people who are using approaches that you would like to know more about		Tamsin's vignettes in other chapters provide some relevant examples.
Supporting access to university-level teaching qualifications	An invitation to give a 15-minute presentation about something they are learning that could be valuable for the teaching team. Support for implementation of improvements they could make based on what they have learnt in their study. Encouragement to include other teachers in these changes.	A chance to share their learning from the study they are undertaking.
Teachers invited to share their learning	Can begin with a presentation. Might expand to working with colleagues to implement improvements they are interested in. Key is that this is supported through: • verbal recognition and other overt recognition • timetabling • teacher release hours.	Includes learning from a range of sources such as: • university and other study as noted above • professional development • personal research • return to industry • an action research project • a community of practice.

Reflective practice

Studies on successful teaching (and success in all professions and occupations) often highlight the importance of reflective practice (see for instance, Schön, 1983; Boud et al., 2006). Supporting the development of reflective practice needs to be undertaken with care. Genuine reflection can be confronting and make people feel vulnerable. Critical reflection needs to be undertaken individually or with trusted colleagues. Forced reflection or required public reflection can result in a performance rather than reflection. There are many ways that an individual or a willing group of trusted colleagues can be supported to undertake reflection (Rushton & Suter, 2012).

In an action research project, the action research team reflects together on the outcomes (informed by analysis) of their changes. Based on this, they then determine together the next changes that they will make. But it is not necessary to be part of an action research project to be able to reflect in a structured way (Rushton & Suter, 2012).

Schön (1983) identifies a range of approaches to reflection, including before and after action. He also has a particular focus on reflection-in-action. Reflection pre-action might include considering what the teacher wants to achieve, and what happened last time in a similar circumstance (such as the last time they taught the same concept). At a basic level, reflection after action considers what happened, and perhaps why it happened. Reflection-in-action refers to changes that can be made while actually doing something. For instance, an accomplished teacher might begin a class based on a well-considered lesson plan, only to realise in-action that some particular prior knowledge needs to be further developed first, or that other circumstances mean the planned approach is no longer likely to be the most valuable. Accomplished teachers usually have an extensive repertoire of teaching approaches they can draw on to enable change due to reflection-in-action.

Brookfield (2017) has done much valuable work related to teacher learning and the learning of adults more broadly. He has also written extensively about reflective practice for teachers. If you do a web search, you can also find videos where he discusses some of the strategies that he suggests. Brookfield identifies four useful lenses for framing reflection: the student lens, the autobiographical lens, peer lens, and articles/books based on relevant research. That is:

- What feedback from, and other information related to, students is there that can inform the reflection?
- What does the feedback from colleagues and peers contribute?
- What do the teacher's prior experiences and present understanding contribute?
- What does the relevant research-based literature contribute?

From a VET and FE perspective, we can also add a fifth lens.

- What does an industry perspective contribute?

Each of these lenses is discussed further below.

Student lens

There are many ways to access the student lens that go beyond the "tick and flick" approach that is often required for student evaluation surveys. This might include one or more of the following:

- in-class discussions about what the students think is working in the subject and any changes that might better support their learning
- consideration of student achievement compared with previous offerings of the subject
- at the end of each class, or of a group of classes, ask students to provide anonymous feedback on:
  - what they have learnt in the class
  - what remains confusing
  - what they would like to learn more about
- group reflection in the last ten minutes of each class about what they learnt
- group discussion at the beginning of each class about what they learnt during the previous lesson.

Colleague lens

Accessing a colleague lens might be as simple as having a chat over a coffee with some trusted colleagues. Alternately, it might be more detailed and sophisticated. It might include approaches such as:

Leading learning

- a detailed discussion at a staff meeting about a particular matter
- a staff survey related to an area of investigation
- scheduled group discussions (weekly, monthly, each semester) related to a particular area of investigation.

Autobiographical lens

This includes your perspective from your experiences as a learner, a worker in the industry you are teaching about, and as a teacher. It is often useful to deliberately reflect on your experiences and understandings from each of those perspectives. However, be careful not to make this the dominant lens; your experiences are just one of the things that should inform your reflections.

Literature/research lens

By reading relevant literature, you can often gain a broader perspective on the issues that you are addressing. Relevant literature can be accessed online, although there is usually a cost for doing so if you do not have access to an academic library. If you are working with a researcher (through an action research project, or other research to support workplace development), the researcher will be able to access relevant literature for you.

Industry lens

For most teaching areas, it can be useful to consider the industry lens from two broad perspectives – large business/organisations, and small-to-medium businesses. Return to industry arrangements as well as regular contact with industry contacts can be valuable in providing this lens. The following are also valuable:

- Many organisations regularly invite industry representatives to contribute to the development of the content that they are teaching.
- Visiting students in their workplace can contribute to the industry lens.
- Inviting students in class to discuss what they are learning in industry.
- Inviting guest speakers from industry.

Survey of your local site

Consider your local site – if there is more than one, it is best to start by considering them separately. The first step in developing a strong trellis of PSLs in a site is determining what already exists. Do the practice architectures enable teacher learning? Does it support the learning of other workers? How might you investigate this further? The questions in Table 8.3 provide a good starting point for a survey of your local site. Often people experience the same site and arrangements in different ways, perhaps because of their different roles, motivations, and experiences. If possible, it is valuable to undertake this survey together with several colleagues, ideally with different roles and experiences. For instance, the Head of School, a qualification coordinator, an accomplished teacher, a novice teacher, a long- term casual teacher, a teacher who teaches only in the evenings. If some of these people are mentors, it will also be valuable to have that perspective.

Table 8.3 Site survey questions

	Initial specific questions to consider	Further questions to consider
Staffroom	• How are the workstations/desks arranged? 　○ For the permanently employed teachers? 　○ For the casually employed teachers? • Is there a communal area that all teachers have easy access to? 　○ Is it used? 　　Could this be made more accessible?	Does anyone, or any group of teachers, have more or less access to accomplished teachers?
Teaching sites	• Is it possible for new teachers to easily observe experienced teachers teaching?	How might new teachers organise to observe an accomplished teacher? How do new or casual teachers know this?
Tearoom	• Is there a staff tearoom? Or a communal table in the staffroom?* • Is it used? When and by who?	If not used, do you know why?

(continued)

Table 8.3 (Cont.)

	Initial specific questions to consider	Further questions to consider

Scheduling	• Is a regular morning tea break scheduled?
	  ○ Who regularly attends?
	  ○ Who doesn't attend?
	  ○ Who is invited to attend?
	• How do they know they are invited?
	
	• Are casual teachers teaching at times when experienced teachers are not available (such as in the evening)?
		How might this impact on:
		• access to discussions with, and advice from, experienced teachers?
		• opportunities to observe experienced teachers doing things such as teaching, developing resources, assessing student learning?

Job design	• Is team teaching supported so that new teachers can teach with experienced teachers? • How is it supported? • What arrangements make it possible? • What arrangements limit team teaching? ○ How might these be overcome?	Team teaching usually combines a range of PSLs: observing others teach, being observed, co-development of resources, reflection before and after teaching, and mentoring. If there is teacher compatibility, team teaching can be (but, of course, is not always) one of the most effective approaches to supporting teacher learning.
	• Does co-teaching occur? (Co-teaching is where two teachers team teach the same subject in the same semester to different cohorts of students.)	What arrangements are in place to support co-teachers to meet and discuss teaching and assessment approaches?
	• Workload	Are accomplished teachers provided with time as part of their total workload to support and/or mentor new and casual teachers?
	• How is the workload associated with volunteerism managed?	What access do new teachers have to experienced teachers? • How does this impact on the workload of experienced teachers? • Do some experienced teachers put up barriers (physical or non-physical) so that they limit contact with casual teachers?

Table 8.3 (Cont.)

	Initial specific questions to consider	Further questions to consider
		○ If so, what other arrangements can be made to ensure new and casual teacher access to advice and support from accomplished teachers? ○ How are accomplished teachers acknowledged and compensated for this additional workload (teaching time release)?

	• Is there evidence of co-development of resources and teaching practices?
	  ○ Who is involved in this co-development?
	  ○ Who is not involved?
	  ○ What time are teachers given for co-development of resources?
	• Does their time allocation change whether or not they engage with co-development of resources?
		Are there arrangements in place that support the co-development of resources and teaching approaches?
		If so, how do new/casual teachers know about this?

Resources	• What resources (such as lesson plans, assessment tasks, teaching resources) are provided to new/casual teachers? • How are new/casual teachers supported to use these resources? • What should new/casual teachers do if they do not know how to use these resources, or if they cannot make sense of them? ○ How do they know this? • What arrangements are there for co-development of resources (also identified in the *Job design* section)?	Is there an assumption that new/casual teachers will know how to use the provided resources?

(*continued*)

Table 8.3 (Cont.)

	Initial specific questions to consider	Further questions to consider
Mentoring	• Is there a mentoring programme?	• Are mentors trained?

	• Who are the mentors?
	   ○ Formal?
	   ○ Informal?
	• Are there any people placed in the role of mentor who would rather not undertake that role?
		• Is mentoring valued?
		• Is it rewarded?

	• How is mentor workload managed?
	   ○ Do mentors receive time release for mentoring or is it in addition to their other work?
		• If someone does not want to be a mentor (or is not suitable as a mentor), what other roles are they expected to undertake instead?
		   ○ Linked to this is whether mentoring is an additional task that gets no compensation.

	• How is induction and induction mentoring arranged?	Good induction can make a real difference to how quickly new teachers can settle into the role.
	• How is developmental mentoring arranged?	Can experienced teachers easily access a mentor in the local site to support their development in specific areas such as teaching in the workplace, online learning? What opportunities are available to support experienced teachers to access appropriate mentors elsewhere?

*This question of how a communal area is used is an important one. As an example, in one of the sites where I undertook research there was a communal area with a communal table that was large enough for all teachers to congregate. Apparently, at one stage there were also sufficient chairs around the table for all. When I visited the site, the table was covered in equipment (used for teaching) and the chairs had made their way to other areas of the staffroom. This communal area was no longer readily available for use as a gathering place for teachers. Further, the research participant noted that only teachers who had a workstation in the staffroom were made welcome in the staffroom (partly because there was nowhere for them to be). Workstations were only available for teachers employed permanently or on contract. This participant went between short-term contracts and casual teaching. He noted that he only felt comfortable being in the staffroom when he was employed on contract.

Concluding comments

This chapter outlines a range of approaches and strategies that can be used to create conditions that support teacher learning in the workplace. Not all will work in every site, and there will be other arrangements specific to your site that may not be successful elsewhere. And, of course, your site will continue to change so that something that did not work, or did not seem possible, a year ago, might work well now. The COVID-19 pandemic has provided a clear illustration of this (Sjølie et al., 2020).

The value of inter-related PSLs is an important concept to keep in mind. When considering changes you might make to your site to better enable teacher learning, also consider how these changes might inter-relate with other PSLs. Well-trained and well-supported mentors can be key to this.

The practice architectures in a site will impact differently on different teachers. In making changes, consider the impact on all, including Fringe Teachers, Favela Teachers, experienced teachers, and accomplished teachers. Because the changes are likely to impact the different groups in different ways, where possible try to set in place arrangements so that none of these groups is overlooked.

Questions to consider

Many relevant questions are included in Table 8.3.

For the individual

- What leading practices are in evidence in your site?
  - Who undertakes those practices?
  - What arrangements constrain others from undertaking those practices in relation to leading teacher learning?
- In your local site, who might make up the team of people to undertake a survey of the PSLs available in your site and the extent to which these PSLs form an inter-related trellis?
- In your local site, who might make up an action research team to undertake a project to develop a trellis of PSLs?

For the organisation

- What leading practices are common in your organisation?
  - What are the practice architectures that prefigure these practices?
- How are middle leaders supported to lead learning?
- Who might be passive resisters to change?
  - What can you learn from these people?

Further reading

Brookfield, S. (2017). *Becoming a critically reflective teacher* (2nd ed.). San Francisco, CA: John Wiley.

Brookfield has a background in adult education. He has written this accessible, easy-to-read book just for teachers.

Rushton, I. & Suter, M. (2012). *Reflective practice for teaching in lifelong learning*. London: Open University Press.

Rushton and Suter provide a range of approaches for reflective practice, from quite basic "technical" reflection to critical reflective approaches.

References

Boud, D., Cressey, P., & Docherty, P. (Eds.) (2006). *Productive reflection at work*. Milton Park: Routledge.

Brookfield, S. (2017). *Becoming a critically reflective teacher* (2nd ed.). San Francisco, CA: John Wiley.

Dymock, D. & Tyler, M. (2018). Towards a more systematic approach to continuing professional development in vocational education and training. *Studies in Continuing Education*, 40(2), 198–211. doi: 10.1080/0158037X.2018.1449102

Edwards-Groves, C., Wilkinson, J., & Mahon, K. (2020). Leading as shared transformative educational practice. In K. Mahon, C. Edwards-Groves, S. Francisco, M. Kaukko, S. Kemmis, & K. Petri. (Eds.), *Pedagogy education and praxis in critical times*. Singapore: Springer.

Francisco, S. (2020). Developing a trellis of practices that support learning in the workplace. *Studies in Continuing Education*, 42(1), 102–117. https://doi.org/10.1080/0158037X.2018.1562439

Grootenboer, P., Edwards-Groves, C., & Rönnerman, K. (2014). Leading practice development: voices from the middle. *Professional Development in Education*. https://doi.org/10.1080/19415257.2014.924985

Kemmis, S., McTaggart, R., & Nixon, R. (2014). *The Action Research Planner: doing critical participatory action research*. Singapore: Springer. https://doi.org/10.1007/978-981-4560-67-2

Kemmis, S., Wilkinson, J., & Edwards Groves, C. (2017). Roads not travelled, roads ahead; how the theory of practice architectures is travelling. In K. Mahon, S. Francisco, & S. Kemmis (Eds.), *Exploring education and professional practice: through the lens of practice architectures*. Singapore: Springer.

Knight, G., White, I., & Granfield, P. (2020). Understanding the Australian Vocational Education and Training workforce. Adelaide: NCVER. www.ncver.edu.au/__data/assets/pdf_file/0044/9659672/Australian-VET-workforce-survey-report.pdf

Olin, A., Francisco, S., Salo, P., Porn, M., & Karlburg-Grenland, G. (2020). Collaborative professional learning for changing educational practices. In K. Mahon, C. Edwards-Groves, S. Francisco, M. Kaukko, S. Kemmis, & K. Petri. (Eds.), *Pedagogy, education, and praxis in critical times*. Singapore: Springer.

Rushton, I. & Suter, M. (2012). *Reflective practice for teaching in lifelong learning*. London: Open University Press.

Schön, D. (1983). *The reflective practitioner*. London: Ashgate.

Sjølie, E., Francisco, S., Kaukko, M., Mahon, K., & Kemmis, S. (2020). Learning in the time of the coronavirus pandemic. *Journal of Praxis in Higher Education*, 2(1), 85–107.

Smeed, J., Kimber, M., Millwater, J., & Ehrich, L. (2009). Power over, with and through: snother look at micropolitics. *Leading and Managing*, 15(1), 26–41.

Smith, E., Yasukawa, K., & Hodge, S. (2015). Australian VET teacher education: what is the benefit of pedagogical studies at university for VET teachers? *TVET@Asia*, Issue 5, July.

Spedding, P. (2020). Re-dressing the balance: practitioner-research as continuing professional development. In M. Gregson and P. Spedding (Eds.), *Practice-focused research in further adult and Vocational Education*, pp. 187–211. Springer Nature.

Wilkinson, J. (2022). *Educational leadership through a practice lens*. Singapore: Springer.

Wilkinson, J. & Kemmis, S. (2015). Practice theory: viewing leadership as leading. *Educational Philosophy and Theory*, 47(4), 342–358. doi: 10.1080/00131857.2014.976928

Wilkinson, J., Olin, A., Lund, T., Ahlberg, A., & Nyvaller, M. (2010). Leading praxis: exploring educational leadership through the lens of practice architectures. *Pedagogy, Culture & Society*, 18(1), 67–79. doi: 10.1080/14681360903556855

So what, now what
Where to from here?

The book began by outlining the high expectations that the community, governments, employers, and students have of Vocational and Further Education (FE) teachers: the varied and extensive skill set required and the need for ongoing learning and development. This chapter brings the book to its conclusion and outlines suggestions for ways forward in enabling teacher learning. In this chapter, you are also introduced to the concept of praxis-informed action. The chapter concludes with a discussion of how to use what you have learnt throughout the book. We begin with an overview of the key messages in the book.

Key messages

Below is a brief overview of the key messages in the book. The purpose of including this section is to pull together some of the main ideas that you have encountered through the book.

Site-based arrangements enable and constrain workplace learning

Workplace learning is not something that happens just because someone is doing their job. It is enabled and constrained because of the arrangements in each local site – the cultural-discursive, material-economic, and social-political arrangements.

The cultural-discursive arrangements enable and constrain the sayings in and about the site. This includes what is said, how it is said, and how things are thought about. Key cultural-discursive arrangements that affect teacher learning include:

So what, now what: where to from here?

- the use of training and education language in the site;
- the use of industry-related language in the site;
- language used (in the site as well as more broadly) in relation to the valuing (or not valuing) of vocational education.

The material-economic arrangements enable and constrain the doings in the site – what is done and how it is done. Key material-economic arrangements that affect teacher learning include:

- the basis on which teachers are employed:
  - Fringe Teachers[1]
  - Favela Teachers
  - teachers employed permanently or on long-term contracts.
- physical arrangements in the staffroom, including access to, and placement of, workstations
- access to a shared tearoom/lunchroom that teachers use
- arrangements related to the observation of, and engagement with, the teaching of others
- availability of resources such as:
  - well-developed lesson plans, assessment tasks, and student resources (for use as part of teaching practices and also as models for the development of similar resources)
  - availability of non-teaching support staff and administration staff
  - easily used and accessible administration systems
  - access to team teaching
- scheduling that enables easy access to other teachers:
  - teaching times (such as evening, daytime) and associated access to teachers for collegial interactions
  - scheduling of a shared time for personal/professional interaction, such as a daily morning tea.

The social-political arrangements enable and constrain the relatings in the site – the relationships of power and solidarity. Key social-political arrangements that affect teacher learning include:

---

1 Note that the terms "Fringe Teacher" and "Favela Teacher" refer to the basis of employment, not to the competency of teachers employed on this basis, or any other aspect of the teachers themselves.

- issues of power:
  - "power over", "power with", and "power through" (discussed in Chapters 4 and 8)
- volunteerism
- solidarity and positive interactions with colleagues.

Even though we often take the arrangements in a site as being relatively fixed, it is worth considering that these arrangements were created by people, and they can be changed by people. Just look at the changes that took place during the pandemic – changes that we could previously not have imagined happening so quickly. The practice architectures changed rapidly and so did the practices they enabled and constrained (Sjolie et al., 2020). In most cases, the arrangements in a site can be changed without the need for such a drastic impetus as a pandemic. Some of these changes can be made quickly and easily. Others will take longer and be more difficult.

The learning of individual teachers is often foregrounded in discussions of teacher development. This can (and often does) lead to the quality of Vocational Education and Training (VET) teaching being considered an issue that relates primarily to individual teachers' actions, skills, and dispositions. In this book, the site-based arrangements that enable and constrain teacher learning have been foregrounded. This emphasis allows organisations, teams, and individuals to become aware of and focus on these arrangements and work toward keeping those arrangements that enable teacher learning and changing those that do not.

In-between spaces that become communicative learning spaces can be valuable in supporting teacher learning

Teachers learn in a range of places. One place of teacher learning that has been highlighted is in in-between spaces – those spaces that are in-between the personal and professional. While in-between spaces are connected with the workplace, they are also a space for personal interactions; in such spaces the focus of conversation moves between work-related and non-work-related discussion. In-between spaces include spaces such as those created by a regularly scheduled morning tea; lunch or morning tea during a professional development (PD) day (how many times have you heard people say they learnt more during the coffee breaks than they did during the PD?);

time together after a formal meeting; a shared car drive to work or between campuses; a regular lunchtime walk with colleagues.

The creation of in-between spaces is not sufficient to ensure teacher learning – they can just be spaces where teachers interact. While this is valuable, it is when an in-between space becomes a communicative learning space that teacher learning occurs. A communicative learning space is one where people interact in a respectful, non-hierarchical way, and where professional learning takes place. Trust and the development of solidarity are important elements of a communicative learning space. Meeting regularly, a shared language (such as a shared industry language), and the telling of stories are also elements that support the development of a communicative learning space. In-between spaces and communicative learning spaces are discussed further in Chapter 7.

Mentoring is important

Mentoring can support teacher learning. We have known this for years. What this book has added is that mentoring can also be a linchpin for the development of a trellis of practices that support learning (PSLs).

While acknowledged as valuable in supporting learning, mentoring can be more or less effective, depending on the skills and practices of the mentor as well as the practice architectures that enable and constrain mentoring in each site (Vignette 5.1 provides a good example of practice architectures constraining good mentoring practices). A mentor training programme that supports the development of mentoring skills and practices is recommended (see Chapter 6). One way to develop mentoring skills is to be a mentor. Another way (which can be combined with the first) is to be mentored. Great mentors can support the development of great mentors.

People can be reluctant to take on a mentoring role. There are a range of reasons for this. One of the key reasons seems to be a lack of confidence in their mentoring skills. I teach a Graduate Diploma subject called Mentoring and Workplace Learning and, at the beginning of the subject, I always ask people to do two things: to get a mentor and become a mentor (this is not compulsory, just recommended). Each of the assignments in the subject has a section where people identify whether they have done either of these things. A large majority of the students taking this subject are experienced teachers. It is therefore surprising how few people become a mentor while they are studying the subject. The explanation usually given for not being a mentor is a lack of skills and experience. In addition to supporting skill development, one of the benefits of a good mentoring programme is that it can help people develop the confidence to be a mentor. If you have been with an organisation even for 12 months (and often less), you can usually be of assistance as an induction mentor. In addition to being of real value for the mentee, this can serve as a relatively easy first step into mentoring for the mentor.

The development of a trellis of practices that support learning (PSLs) can be powerful in enabling teacher learning in the workplace

Teachers engage in many PSLs. When PSLs inter-relate with each other, a trellis of PSLs develops. Generally, the more inter-related PSLs there are, the stronger the trellis, and the greater the support for teacher learning (see Figures 5.2 and 5.5). This is not always the case. See Figure 5.3 for an example of a trellis with many inter-related PSLs that is relatively fragile. In this trellis, the individual PSLs are each of limited timespan, many occur infrequently, and many of them are not ongoing – so the teacher has to actively seek out the PSLs each time. As a result, this trellis of PSLs is not as strong in supporting teacher learning as some others with less inter-related PSLs. It is useful to turn this around to consider that, in a strong trellis of PSLs, many (or even all) of the PSLs are easily accessed, available regularly and for extended periods, not always reliant on the individual teacher to ensure their availability, and each separately provides good support for teacher learning.

Mentoring is usually the linchpin of a strong trellis of PSLs. An experienced and highly skilled mentor can often work together with others to create a strong trellis of PSLs.

Leading teacher learning involves working with others to enhance and change site-based arrangements

A crucial aspect of leading teacher learning involves working together with others to identify what site-based arrangements enable and constrain teacher learning. This is followed by making changes to, where possible, enhance those arrangements that enable teacher learning and transform those arrangements that constrain teacher learning. Changing site-based arrangements can enable different practices to occur. This is not usually a quick fix. To complicate things, some arrangements that enable one teacher's learning may not enable the learning of another. Arrangements for supporting the learning of casually employed teachers might need to be considered separately to arrangements for the learning of experienced teachers.

Leading teacher learning is rarely a one-person exercise – it usually involves the deliberate and active engagement of the people involved. Leading practices that focus on "power with" and "power through" (see Chapter 8) are likely to encourage and motivate teachers to work together to make positive changes. Such approaches support the development of teacher agency.

Changing site-based arrangements can be transformational. It can also be complicated, and take time, energy, and commitment. Positive and sustained transformation usually requires a nuanced and reflective approach that continues to change and develop. Action research, undertaken by a self-selected and motivated team of people directly involved in the changes, can be valuable in supporting such an approach (see Chapter 8).

Developing praxis

Research shows that when first learning to be a teacher the focus is often on survival – getting through the day, the week, and the semester. This usually involves learning the content that forms the basis for the teaching and determining "how things work in this place at this time". As teachers become more confident in their basic knowledge and understanding, they often step back and reflect on what they are doing and why they are doing it. They also often consider how they can make a difference – for their students, the industry that they are teaching about, and sometimes the community that they are a part of (local, national, international, and global). Once teachers begin asking themselves these questions, they are starting to develop praxis (Mahon et al., 2020). (Stay with me here – there is just a brief introduction to some philosophy before we get to actions.)

There are two main traditions of praxis, one that follows from Aristotle's teaching and relates to action that is morally informed. Kemmis et al. (2014) identify this as "action that aims for the good of those involved and for the good of humankind" (p. 26). The other tradition is based on the works of Marx and Hegel. This tradition relates to action that aims to change society – often referred to as history-making action. (I bet you did not expect to read about the philosophies of Aristotle, Hegel, and Marx when you started reading this book!) "'Educational praxis,' therefore, may be understood in two ways: first as educational action that is morally committed and informed by traditions in the field ('right conduct'), and second, as history-making educational action" (Kemmis et al., 2014, p. 26). Both these understandings are relevant for VET and FE teachers.

We can understand the purpose of VET and FE to be to "prepare people to live well in a world worth living in" (Kemmis et al., 2014, p. 27). What "living well in a world worth living in" actually involves is open to interpretation. Both are usually taken to relate to operating in a morally informed way. Preparing people to live well includes preparing students to be ethical and professional members of their industry. As Brennan Kemmis (2008) argues, "Vocational Education and Training was, and continues to be, about developing the skills and knowledge appropriate for a specific trade or industry, and about the 'virtues' associated with the trade – virtues like perseverance, reliability, precision, honesty and ethical behaviour" (p. 196). I hear similar things from the teachers who are participants in my research. For instance, Michael, who you have come across throughout the book, and whose words (quoted again below) you read at the beginning of the book.

I want to give the students as much as I can so they can go out confidently and do a great job and be fulfilled and happy. And for the employer, so they can be absolutely confident that if they employ that person, they know what they are doing.

In many other ways, Michael, and many of the participants in my research, referred to the "virtues" that they hoped to support students to develop. An important part of what these teachers do is support their students to become valued members of their industry who operate ethically, morally, and professionally. As Brennan Kemmis (2008) argues:

Praxis as it developed in the traditional apprenticeship model clearly survives in the work and conduct of many contemporary VET teachers and trainers. These teachers and trainers continue to reassert the moral and ethical dimensions and responsibilities of the work itself and the contributions that their students can make as morally informed participants in the communities into which their students will go as qualified and credentialled members. They model in their teaching and training those conditions under which the development of moral reasoning accompanies the acquisition of skills.

(p. 204)

Teachers need to continue to be supported to be able to do this, and it is leaders in the local site (the workplace), as well as leaders across an organisation and the Vocational Education field, who can create conditions for this support. As Wilkinson et al. (2010) argue, "educational leaders ... [are] the key 'architects of practice architectures' [and] are in a position to influence the conditions in which praxis may flourish" (p. 67). Research (Francisco et al., 2021) has shown that three key components in supporting the development of praxis are power, trust, and agency. Leading that relies on "power with" and "power through" (see Chapter 8) can support the development of trust and enable teacher agency. See the *Further reading* section if you want to follow this up.

Educational praxis can be seen as forming, self-forming, and transforming (Mahon et al., 2020). It can be forming in that it involves action that is deliberately aimed at forming the students we work with so that they carry on the ethical values and principles of the trade/industry we are teaching about. It can be self-forming through reflection and development of understanding about the impact of our actions and the actions of others. Mahon et al. (2020) characterise the self-forming dimension of praxis in the following way:

It is self-forming in the sense that actors gain knowledge (including self-understanding and understanding of their world) as they become aware of the consequences of what they are doing in practice, and this in turn, orients and informs their ongoing action in a way that shapes their being and becoming as actors.

(p. 30)

And it can be transforming in that a praxis approach can serve to transform ourselves, our students, and even the industries that we teach about so that we are able to "live well in a world worth living in" (Kemmis et al., 2014, p. 27).

Now what? Where to from here?

Well, that depends on what you want to do in relation to supporting the workplace learning of teachers, the scope of your vision, and what is possible given your circumstances. Do you want to make changes to an entire organisation? A teaching department? A small teaching team? To your own workplace learning? What, realistically, is possible for you, at this time, and in this place?

Whole-of-organisation level changes

If you are planning to make changes at a whole-of-organisation level, and if the organisation is a large one, there are many factors to consider. In a large organisation, a project management approach is likely to be needed at the organisational level. This will probably include a communication strategy, a risk management strategy, a budget, an implementation strategy, an evaluation strategy, a timeline, and a plan to get engagement by teachers, other employees, managers, and leaders. Senior manager sponsorship will also be valuable. What is needed in each site, how it is implemented in each site, and what is done in each site cannot be determined by the organisational project manager, or by a group of senior managers. Such an approach might create an outcome, but it is unlikely to be the most appropriate outcome for each site. So, to be explicit, if the practice architectures of an organisation are to be transformed to better enable the workplace learning of teachers, such arrangements will look different in each local site. Further, the changes will need to be actively owned and led in each site by the people who work in that site (what that might involve is discussed further below).

Having noted strongly that changes for each site will need to be determined by those working in each local site, there is also a lot that can take place at the organisational level. The development and support for a whole-of-organisation mentoring programme is one such strategy. Another is establishing a fund that can be used to support (clearly justified) changes identified by a teaching department. At the beginning of the project, a useful strategy to get others engaged and motivated is to support a pilot programme. The pilot should be undertaken by a teaching area that is keen to trial changes that increase support for teachers' workplace learning. Mentoring those who are leading changes in each workplace can be valuable. Also valuable are regularly scheduled meetings where leaders who are implementing changes to workplace arrangements can meet to share what their teams are doing and seek inspiration, advice and support from each other.

An evaluation strategy needs to be developed at the same time as the implementation strategy. One important purpose of developing an

So what, now what: where to from here?

evaluation strategy is so that all stakeholders can agree on what success looks like. Often with a large project, different stakeholders have clear ideas about what success will look like, and each makes assumptions that everyone else has the same understanding of what that is. Success can look very different to different people. Early work on agreeing what success looks like can be important in ensuring that the project is considered successful. An evaluation strategy for the whole organisation will necessarily focus on broad outcomes so that it does not reduce flexibility for the areas putting the projects into place.

As noted, one important whole-of-organisation strategy that can be implemented is the development of a mentoring programme. Chapter 6 provides more information about factors to consider in implementing a mentoring programme. One of the benefits of having a mentoring programme is that more people will become mentors, and more people will become mentees – this also includes people who are not part of the mentoring programme. A whole-of-organisation mentoring programme, especially one that includes mentor training, can positively impact the culture of an organisation beyond the mentoring programme itself.

Teaching department, or small organisation, level changes

If you are part of a large teaching department, it might be that the whole-of-organisation approach discussed above will be most appropriate for your department. But for most teaching departments such an approach will not be necessary. Nonetheless, some of the broader strategies might be useful to consider. This includes setting up a mentoring programme (if there is not already a whole-of-organisation programme that meets the needs of your department). Gaining senior management sponsorship can also be valuable, particularly in supporting access to funds to make identified changes, as well as agreement to such changes if such agreement is required. Another strategy discussed in the whole-of-organisation section that is also useful at the department level is developing an evaluation plan to ensure that those involved agree on what success will look like.

For most teaching departments, the strategies outlined in Chapter 8 will be appropriate for your team. This includes developing a team of volunteers to work together to determine what practice architectures in the workplace enable and constrain teacher learning, what arrangements should stay the same, and what changes might be made in the short, medium and long term to better enable teacher learning in the workplace. As Chapter 8 suggests, an action research project undertaken by teachers to improve teacher learning in the workplace (or several projects being undertaken by several teams) is recommended. Such an approach can usefully begin with a survey of the site – the questions outlined in Table 8.3 are a good start for such a survey.

Small teaching team

A small group of committed teachers working together can make a big difference in their workplace. Such a group could use the strategies outlined in Chapter 8, beginning with the workplace survey, and then identifying appropriate short-, medium- and long-term changes. An action research approach would be a valuable way to progress these changes and make them sustainable.

Individual – supporting your learning and the learning of colleagues

Using the learning that you have done through reading this book, what can you do to support your workplace learning and the workplace learning of colleagues? In short, a lot.

As the concept of a trellis of PSLs illustrates, inter-related PSLs are more powerful than isolated PSLs. For individuals, one important first step you can take is to get a mentor. Another is to become a mentor – mentors usually report that they have learnt as much through being a mentor as mentees have. Introducing your mentor to the concept of a trellis of PSLs can be an important step for you and your mentor in working together to create such a trellis.

If you are an accomplished teacher, you will have a wealth of experience to draw on to provide a framework for developing an individual trellis of PSLs. Tamsin's example (see Vignettes 5.4, 7.6, and 7.8) illustrates how an accomplished teacher, even when largely isolated and with limited support from her organisation for her ongoing learning, was able to develop a trellis of PSLs. Imagine what she could have done if her organisation had actively created practice architectures that enabled rather than constrained her learning. It is important to highlight that Tamsin's relative success in supporting her own learning, when there were so many arrangements that constrained that learning, is relatively unique. Two other participants in my research who were isolated, and whose organisations provided limited

So what, now what: where to from here?

support for their learning, did not fare as well. We can be inspired by Tamsin, but such an approach should not be considered the basis for a plan except in extreme circumstances. Instead, for isolated teachers such as Tamsin (for instance, teachers who are the only ones in their teaching area on a campus, or for teachers who teach only in the evening when their colleagues teach only during the day), providing regular, scheduled, and sustained opportunities for teachers to interact and reflect with other teachers is crucial.

As noted throughout the book, interactions with colleagues are important in supporting teacher learning. As an individual, a powerful way that you can support your learning, as well as that of others, is to work together with trusted colleagues to create the workplace environment that can support your learning. An action research project can provide a good focus for such work.

Concluding comments

The book began with quotes from some of the teachers who participated in my research: they showed the passion the teachers felt for teaching and supporting student learning. Most of the teachers who I have interacted with have a real commitment to supporting students – not just as workers (or future workers), but as people: people who are part of our community; people who are part of creating the world in which we live, and who will be part of creating the future.

I leave you with the quotes from teachers that the book began with.

I love teaching in VET. I'm doing it because I do love it and I feel like I've found my place.

Maria, Business teacher

I want to give the students as much as I can so they can go out confidently and do a great job and be fulfilled and happy. And for the employer, so they can be absolutely confident that if they employ that person, they know what they are doing. I would have been a teacher for all my life if I'd known how nice and intellectually stimulating it is.

Michael, Horticulture teacher

The biggest emotion I feel in my teaching is the pride that I feel for the students. You know, when they physically create something practical, or when I set them tasks to deliberately challenge them, and they meet the challenge. So, a lot of pride there. I really enjoy it; I'm really happy doing it.

Ewan, Air Conditioning and Refrigeration teacher

I'm passionate about teaching…I love working out how to engage disengaged students, and to make a difference to their lives.

Tamsin, Foundation Studies teacher

It is teachers such as these who are teaching students to live well and operate within their industry in an ethical way. Together with their students they can also help to create a world worth living in. It is our responsibility, and our privilege, to support them, ourselves, and each other, to do so.

Questions to consider

For the organisation

- What is the present capacity of your organisation to make short-term and medium-term changes that enable teacher learning?
  - What needs to change, and what sponsorship might be useful to increase that capacity?
- What changes can you make right now to better enable teacher learning in the workplace?
  - What will you do this week to progress this?

For the individual

- What can you do right now to begin to implement what you have learnt in this book?
  - What will you do this week to progress this?

Further reading

Brennan Kemmis, R. (2008). Freedom for praxis: an unburied and unforgotten tradition. In S. Kemmis & T. Smith (Eds.), *Enabling praxis*. Rotterdam: Sense.

So what, now what: where to from here?

In this chapter, Brennan Kemmis provides an interesting discussion of praxis and praxis development in VET in Australia. It is a valuable chapter that I wish every VET teacher and VET leader could read. It is getting a bit old now, and therefore more difficult to access. If you are interested in reading the chapter and are having trouble accessing it, please get in touch with me at sfrancisco@csu.edu.au and I can help you get a copy.

Francisco, S., Forssten Seiser, A., & Grice, C. (2021). Professional learning that enables the development of critical praxis. *Professional Development in Education*, 1–15. doi:10.1080/19415257.2021.1879228

If you are interested in finding out more about some of the key factors involved in professional learning that support the development of praxis for teachers (spoiler alert: key factors are power, trust, and agency), this is a good starting point.

Mahon, K., Heikkinen, H. L. T., Huttanen, R., Boyle, T., & Sjølie, E. (2020). In K. Mahon, C. Edwards-Groves, S. Francisco, M. Kaukko, S. Kemmis, & K. Petri. (Eds.), *Pedagogy, education, and praxis in critical times*. Singapore: Springer.

If you are interested in finding out more about praxis, this is a good starting point.

References

Brennan Kemmis, R. (2008). Freedom for praxis: An unburied and unforgotten tradition. In S. Kemmis & T. Smith (Eds.), *Enabling Praxis*. Rotterdam: Sense.

Francisco, S., Forssten Seiser, A., & Grice, C. (2021). Professional learning that enables the development of critical praxis. *Professional Development in Education*, 1–15. doi:10.1080/19415257.2021.1879228

Kemmis, S., Wilkinson, J., Edwards-Groves, C., Grootenboer, P., Hardy, I., & Bristol, L. (2014). *Changing practices, changing education*. Singapore: Springer. doi: 10.1007/978-981-4560-47-4

Mahon, K., Heikkinen, H. L. T., Huttanen, R., Boyle, T., & Sjølie, E. (2020). In K. Mahon, C. Edwards-Groves, S. Francisco, M. Kaukko, S. Kemmis & K. Petri. (Eds.), *Pedagogy, education, and praxis in critical times*. Singapore: Springer.

Sjølie, E., Francisco, S., Kaukko, M., Mahon, K., & Kemmis, S. (2020). Learning in the time of the Coronavirus pandemic. *Journal of Praxis in Higher Education*, 2(1), 85–107.

Wilkinson, J., Olin, A., Lund, T., Ahlberg, A., & Nyvaller, M. (2010). Leading praxis: exploring educational leadership through the lens of practice architectures. *Pedagogy Culture and Society*, 18(1), 67–79. https://doi.org/10.1080/14681360903556855

Index

accomplished teachers 34–35, 39, 148–149, 153–154, 155–157
action research 144–146; team 145–146, 173
adult learning principles 99–101, 110
agency 68–70, 123–126, 140–141, 173

casually employed teachers 6, 23–28, 33, 34, 46, 48, 70, 87, 116–118, 147–152; access to professional development 6, 48; Favela Teachers 25, 147–152, 169; Fringe Teachers 26, 147–152, 169
communicative learning spaces 126–133, 133–135, 170–171
cultural-discursive arrangements 44, 45–47, 55, 58–59, 62–63, 111, 168–169; industry language 46, 55; training and education language 46–47, 55; developmental mentoring 91, 95–97

developmental mentoring 95–97
doings 45, 47, 143, 147, 169

ecologies of practices 76
e-mentoring 104–105

Favela Teachers 25, 147–152, 169
Fringe Teachers 26, 147–152, 169

how to go on 6–7, 31

in-between spaces 115–135, 170–171; casually employed teachers 116–117, 120–122
induction mentoring 91–95, 164

leading teacher learning 138–140, 172–173, 175–176; casually employed teachers 147–152; experienced and accomplished teachers 153–157
learning 6–7; situated 7; workplace 4–7

material-economic arrangements 45, 47–51, 56–57, 59–60, 63, 169; employment arrangements 47–49; physical arrangements 49; resources 49–50; team teaching

50–51, 57, 61; scheduling 51; staff turnover 48–49, 58, 60, 61, 118
mentoring 61, 87–88, 90–112, 171; adult learning principles 99–101, 109, 110–111; developmental mentoring 91, 95–97; e-mentoring 104–105; formal 97–98; induction mentoring 91–95; informal 97–98; learning goals 98, 100, 101–102, 103; peer group mentoring 107; phases of a mentoring relationship 101–104; specialist 106–107; supervisors as mentors 107; volunteerism 58, 106, 111
mentoring programme 98–101, 176–177; mentor development 99, 108–111
mentors 91, 142, 178; specialising in particular areas 106–107; skills and characteristics 108–109
middle leaders 140–141

novice teachers 46–47; learning 32–34, 47, 49–50, 52, 148, 150–152

peer group mentoring 107
phases of a mentoring relationship 101–104; preparation 101; negotiation 101–102; mentoring for growth 102–103; closure and redefinition 103–104
power 48, 52–53, 139–140, 175, 169–170, 173, 175; power over 52–53; power through 53, 57; power with 53

practice architectures 53–68, 139, 143–144, 147, 149, 154, 170, 171, 175, 176, 177; changing 143–144; 155–157; that enable and constrain mentoring 111
practices 7, 8, 31, 32, 33, 34, 44, 46, 52, 68–69, 75–76, 139–142
practices that support learning 75–76, 78, 79–80, 84–86, 142, 150–152, 155–157; online 81–83
praxis 173–175, 181; praxis-informed action 174–175
professional development: access 6, 33, 35, 48, 147–148; accomplished teachers 153–157

reflective practice 158–160
relatings 45, 51, 143, 147, 169

sayings 44, 45, 143, 147, 168
site survey 70, 142–143, 161–164, 178
social-political arrangements 45, 48, 51–53, 57–58, 60–61, 64–65, 111, 146, 169–170; power 52–53; solidarity 58; inclusion/exclusion 48, 52, 58, 70

teacher agency 123–126, 140–141, 173
teacher employment arrangements 47–49; *see also* Favela Teachers; Fringe Teachers
teacher learning 69; enabling and constraining 46, 47, 54, 70
teacher role 7

Index

teacher turnover 48–49, 56, 60–61
teacher workload 33, 37, 49, 50, 53–54, 93, 95, 96, 106, 162–164
teaching qualifications 153–154
team teaching 37, 38, 50–51, 57, 61, 79, 80, 152, 156, 162, 169
theory of practice architectures 8, 10, 44–53

trellis of practices that support learning 40, 75–88, 90, 141–143, 172

volunteerism 49, 53–54, 58, 106, 162, 170

workplace learning 4–5, 37, 148, 168–170; limitations 4–5, 6

Printed in the United States
by Baker & Taylor Publisher Services